MW01289607

Advance Praise for *The Irony of Grace:*

The Irony of Grace is a must-read, a powerfully dramatic story of two tragic collisions—one fueling bitter resentments and the other igniting smoldering regrets. Tragedy turned to triumph when a humble family in a buggy offered what seemed unthinkable—an amazing gift of forgiveness that shattered the stranglehold of bitterness and self-condemnation.

Having been rescued from a burning vehicle ten seconds before it exploded, I am a survivor of being hit by a drunk, wrong-way driver on the freeway. Texting while driving has become a tragedy equaling drunk driving, and Chandler Gerber tells his texting story with remarkable integrity. This story grips me every time I get behind the wheel of my car. This book should be required reading for anyone with a driver's license.

-Dave Beckwith, pastor and author of *THE EDGE: God's Power Perfected in Weakness*

Chandler's story is truly one of finding yourself one day in the lowest valley imaginable and then climbing back out with the help of faith, family and friends to experience fullness and purpose while realizing that everything happens for a reason. He teaches us that amazing things can happen if you allow yourself to be vulnerable enough to change personally and spiritually. Chandler's faith and the encouragement of those closest to him have allowed him to gain new meaning and purpose for his life forever moving forward. I encourage everyone who reads this book to take his advice and life messages seriously, as he has lived through misery, but now is turning it into an incredible victory of change and awareness for himself and so many more.

-Chandler Harnish, Former NFL Quarterback

"With piercing honesty, Chandler Gerber shares his testimony of God's faithfulness in the midst of a tragedy. *The Irony of Grace* is a powerful and moving story that will linger in your mind and in your heart long after you close the book."

-Suzanne Woods Fisher, bestselling author of *Amish Peace: Simple Wisdom for a Complicated World*

When a person, whose decision to text while driving kills three people, takes full responsibility for his careless choice, we need to heed his words: No text is so important it's worth putting others and yourself at risk. Thank you, Chandler Gerber, for not burying your past, but for using it to potentially save lives and to put God's forgiveness and restoration on display.

-Lynne Ford, Radio host of the 'Mid-Morning' program on 90.3 WBCL

The Irony of Grace

A Journey of Forgiveness

Chandler Gerber

© 2016, Chandler Gerber

All rights reserved. No part of this publication may be reproduced, stored in a retrieval system, or transmitted in any form or by any means—electronic, mechanical, photo-copying, recording, or otherwise—without the prior written permission of the publisher. The only exception is brief quotations in printed reviews. For information, please address Hartline Literary Agency; 123 Queenston Drive; Pittsburgh, Pennsylvania 15235.

All Scripture quotations, unless otherwise indicated, are taken from the Holy Bible, New International Version®, NIV®. Copyright ©1973, 1978, 1984, 2011 by Biblica, Inc.™ Used by permission of Zondervan. All rights reserved worldwide. www.zondervan.com The "NIV" and "New International Version" are trademarks registered in the United States Patent and Trademark Office by Biblica, Inc.™

Special Thanks
to Jerry Gramckow for all of his help
in writing this book

Foreword

I had first been introduced to Chandler Gerber the same way you probably were—through a national ad campaign for anti-texting-and-driving, funded by AT&T and directed by the brilliant filmmaker Werner Herzog. The short film featured four lives that were impacted by texting while driving. Of the four stories, Chandler's was the one I couldn't shake off, it was *that* poignant, *that* transparent. And it's had a lasting impact on me. If I'm ever tempted to take out my phone while I'm driving, my mind jumps to that sunny morning in Indiana, to that tragic outcome of Chandler's situation. And then I keep my phone in my purse.

Two years ago, I tracked down Chandler to see if he would be willing to be interviewed for a non-fiction book I was working on about forgiveness through examples of the Amish. Chandler was remarkably accessible, quick to respond, and open to an interview. The forgiveness offered by the Amish family who suffered most from that tragic car accident was genuine, powerful, healing, and restorative. I wasn't surprised by their response to him. The Amish take forgiveness seriously, believing that forgiving others has eternal significance. Their example shows us what Christ meant in the Lord's Prayer: "For if ye forgive men their trespasses, your heavenly Father will also forgive you: But if ye forgive not men their trespasses, neither will your

Father forgive your trespasses" (Matt 6:14-15, KJV). Yes, the ready forgiveness of the Amish family in Chandler's story is a mighty example.

But there was another powerful message in Chandler's story, and it came from deep inside him: his response under questioning in the midst of a chaotic emergency. After the accident, as police arrived and traffic was gridlocked, he sat in a friend's car, waiting to be questioned by the police. *Chandler,* he thought to himself, *be honest. You were being careless. You caused this. You have to take responsibility for this.*

Chandler told the truth, though it would have been easy, understandable, even advisable, to refuse to talk without an attorney present. No one would have blamed him if he refused to answer the police officer's questions on the spot or if he had insisted on having a lawyer present. No one would have blamed him for omitting—not necessarily lying, just not volunteering—the fact that he had been texting while driving. In fact, that's exactly what most of us would do if we found ourselves in a similar situation. Denial is an automatic reaction; offering excuses would be natural. Chandler could have lied.

But something rose up in Chandler in that critical moment that was bigger and more significant to him than the instinct of self-protection. His faith intersected with his circumstances.

"I didn't want to lie," Chandler said. "As a follower of Christ, I had to take responsibility for it." He felt as if God was telling him, "You've talked a good game. When the heat turns up, are you going to turn and run?"

Chandler couldn't contradict his walk as a Christian, despite the consequences. And those consequences might have been pretty severe. He knew he could be facing years in prison for the death of three Amish children, despite the fact that it was an accident.

Chandler Gerber didn't lie. He told the truth. And that's why he has the right to tell us his story. He has something important to teach all of us, and we have something to learn from this young man. In that blink of an eye, Chandler put his trust in God. Not in a clever lawyer, not in a policeman's report, but in God's ability to redeem any and all circumstances for good (Romans 8:28).

God did not minimize or excuse Chandler's unfortunate choice to text and drive on that sunny morning. The consequences were very real. But He did start Chandler on the long work of redemption. He did restore him.

We will all face moments of crisis in our life—consequences of our own doing or the effects of someone else's. How will you respond in moments of crisis? How will I? How will our faith affect our decisions in those moments? Chandler's story will inspire you to make the right decision now, *before* you need it, so you can draw on a deep reservoir of faith when you do need it. *The Irony of Grace* will help you find your own reservoir.

Suzanne Woods Fisher
Author of *The Heart of the Amish: Life Lessons on Peacemaking and the Power of Forgiveness*
San Francisco, California

One

My head snapped up when I heard the explosion. Shards of glass rained down on me and all around me as I brought the company van to a stop. I could hardly see through what remained of the windshield, but I could see enough to know that what slid down the front of the van from the roof was a limp human body.

"I love you." Those were the last three words I'd texted my wife just as the van I was driving smashed into the back of an Amish buggy at sixty miles per hour. No skid marks. No swerving at the last second. I never saw it. I tried to suppress the sense, the almost-certain knowledge, that I'd just killed someone.

What happened? What in the world was that? Myriad feelings flashed through my mind in that instant. Mingled among the jumbled, rapid-fire thoughts was a sense that my heart rate was horrifyingly rapid. It felt like a lifetime went by before the van came to a stop, but at the same time it felt like a microsecond. Time became random. Reality became chaotic. But when the realization that I almost certainly had hit and killed someone became inescapable, I nearly vomited.

"What have I done?" I mulled repeatedly. I sat in the van for a few seconds as I gathered my thoughts. Then I forced myself to open the door and step out. I didn't want to walk around the van and see what I'd done, but I knew I had to face it. Before I did, I punched the side of the van as hard as I could and screamed an obscenity. Not my proudest moment as a follower of Christ, but my emotions got the better of me.

I walked to the back of the van and froze at the sight. In the ditch, an Amish family lay unconscious and sprawled out around a dying horse and a crumpled buggy. It looked like a set for a movie scene. It didn't seem real. *Please, God,* I pleaded in my thoughts, *it can't be real.* The mother was on her hands and knees, face down in the grass. The impact had knocked her off her seat with so much force that she appeared to be in the same position she'd been in while sitting in the buggy.

That part of State Road 124 is normally very busy. At that moment, however, it was empty. I was surrounded by complete silence as I gazed upon the destruction I'd just caused. I wanted to run, and not stop running until I was in another country, because I knew I'd just made the worst mistake of my life. Instead of running from the problem, though, I decided to face it head on, right then. I grabbed my phone, the one I'd been texting on when I hit the buggy, and called 911.

The operator answered with the standard response: "911 dispatch, what's the emergency?"

"I need ambulances out here on State Road 124 between Bluffton and Monroe! I just hit an Amish buggy, and I think I killed people," I yelled into the phone.

I was still on the phone as a few cars came upon the scene and people jumped out to see what had happened. The operator asked some more questions that I can't even remember because I was sobbing and trying to multi-task.

I was trying to talk to the operator, talk to the people who were pulling up to the accident scene, and still trying to process everything. At some point I hung up and quickly called three people in succession. I called my wife, my dad, and Shawn, my co-worker, in that order. "I need you out here between Country Church Road and Monroe on 124! I just hit an Amish buggy and I think I killed people!"

All of them had the same response. "Oh my gosh. Okay, I'll be right there."

Telling my wife, Rachel, was the hardest of the three calls. I knew she was half asleep, stressed with her pregnancy, and prior to the call, unaware of where I even was. Rachel is a strong woman though. She later told me that when I called her she just collapsed onto the couch and began sobbing. Her hormones were already all over the place because of the pregnancy, and then this wake-up call was more than she felt capable of handling. She called her mom and couldn't even get the words out of her mouth because of the uncontrollable crying. When she finally was able to speak, her mom calmly replied that things would work out, it was just an accident. "He was texting!" Rachel sobbed into the phone.

"Okay, let me come pick you up, and we will go out and see how things are. We have no idea," my mother-in-law replied. When they came upon the crash scene, all they could see were lights, cars, and people everywhere. They had to walk for what seemed like miles before finally spotting me, sobbing in the middle of the road.

The scene appeared chaotic, which is just how I felt.

As I stood there and watched the drama unfold, two men walked up to me. I was sobbing uncontrollably as I declared, "I'm screwed!" I knew texting and driving was illegal in Indiana, but I'd chosen to do it anyway. When that law was passed, just a bit more than nine months before the accident, I'd thought it was one of the dumbest pieces of legislation ever. As I looked at the carnage I'd caused, I realized why the law had been passed.

One of the men quietly replied: "Why? It was just an accident."

I chose right then and there to be honest. "I was texting! It's illegal to text and drive." Both men looked at me wide-eyed, as if to say, "Oh boy, you might be in some big trouble here."

At that point I just sat down in the middle of the road and stared as far as I could see in every direction. Everywhere I turned, I saw people running, emergency vehicles with lights flashing, and commotion. In my panic I went emotionally numb.

When my dad called my mom about the Amish buggy accident, she was grocery shopping at Wal-Mart. She left her full cart

The Indiana Law

The Indiana law against texting while driving says, "A person may not use a telecommunications device to:

(1) type a text message or an electronic mail message;

(2) transmit a text message or an electronic mail message; or

(3) read a text message or an electronic mail message;

while operating a moving motor vehicle unless the device is used in conjunction with hands free or voice operated technology, or unless the device is used to call 911 to report a bona fide emergency."

in the bread aisle and ran out to her car. The whole way to the accident scene she was praying over and over, "Please help him, please help him." When she arrived, she had to park behind a line of cars that were stopped on 124. She pulled into the grass in the ditch and started running. She had to run, probably half a mile or more, right through the actual accident site, to reach where I was sitting in someone's van.

The police told her to stop when she got to them, but she was crying as she pleaded, "It was my son who hit them! Please, let me go to him!" They looked at her compassionately and said to go ahead but just be careful. It was a horrific scene to have to literally pass through and see up close. She just wanted to get to me to try to comfort me, calm me down, and find out what in the world had happened. So many people were lined up and out of their cars that it almost made us claustrophobic. My parents immediately texted both of my brothers so that they did not hear about the accident from others, but rather, they were able to hear the story from our family directly. My middle brother was away at college with finals, and could not get home for a few days. It was terribly hard on him not being there with all of us. My youngest brother was in class at school and came home right away.

My co-worker, Shawn, arrived about ten minutes after I called him. His wife, Mindy, just happened to be traveling down that same road at the same time. They pulled up from different directions, and Mindy walked up to me and gave me a big hug. I can still see Shawn's face as he surveyed the scene. He was in shock, too, from what I could see.

A couple other people I knew happened to be there around that time too, and were trying to calm me. A great family friend, a man named Greg, had been farming in the field directly beside where the accident happened. He later told me he heard an explosion-like sound, so he looked up and couldn't believe what he saw. He, along with some others, got me to another van and sat me down in the passenger seat. I looked ahead at people trying to help the family in the ditch to my left. I spotted my dad then, walking toward the van I was sitting in, and at that moment I felt like a big failure, even though I'd been married several years and had a family of my own. I knew I'd brought shame and embarrassment on our family.

My dad walked up and gave me a big hug as I sobbed and told him, "I'm so sorry. I'm so sorry. It was an accident." In all the turmoil, I only vaguely remember my wife and mother-in-law arriving. I think Rachel was also in shock.

I'd heard stories like this on the news and thought, "Wow, that's too bad." And then I flipped to another channel. I couldn't flip to another channel this time though. This was real. This was my life—and several other lives. My dad said a prayer with me then, and he prayed for the family I'd hit, and for whatever was going to come in the following days and weeks.

At that point, enough time had passed for Dio, the investigating officer, to arrive at the scene. He was a compassionate guy who was trying to get some answers out of me so he could piece together what had happened. But I was in shock and could barely talk, so I wasn't making his job any easier. At times I'd calm down enough to answer a question or two, but then I'd lose it again. The straw that broke the camel's back was when I saw a hearse slowly drive by the van I was sitting in. I knew at that moment, without a doubt, that I was responsible for at least one fatality.

Officer Hernandez had left to talk to some others at the scene. He returned and resumed questioning me. I told him exactly what happened. "I was driving east, texting with my wife, and then I remember an explosion sound when I hit the buggy. It was the windshield breaking, the front of the van crumpling, and the buggy being splintered to pieces."

He told me it was standard protocol for any driver who was responsible for an accident like that to have blood work done to check for alcohol or drug use. I complied, knowing the only things that had hindered my driving that morning were the sun in my eyes and my texting. My mother-in-law and my wife drove me to the local hospital for blood work. I could hardly believe that a little bit before I was on my way to work, and the next thing I knew I was going for blood work to see if I was on any drugs or narcotics at the time of the accident. It was a quiet ride. We pulled into the hospital and I made my way into the emergency room for the tests.

A police officer was there to oversee the situation, so I asked him what was going to happen.

"It was an accident," he replied. "It was bad, but things happen."

"I was texting while I was driving," I told him.

"Oh, well, that changes things," he replied. He didn't give me details, but it appeared I was in big trouble, even with no drugs or alcohol in my system.

As I knew it would, the blood work came back clean, and I was released. We went to my parents' house and hunkered down. My grandparents, my youngest brother, and other family and friends were all there at different times, and a minister from my church stopped by and prayed with our family.

"Dio Hernandez will be coming by," my dad told me later that day. "He has to ask some more questions, and he wants to look at your phone. Two little kids passed away at the scene, a three-year-old, and a five-year-old. The mother and another son were taken by helicopter to a hospital in Fort Wayne." My heart sank even further than I thought possible. Little did I know that things were about to get much worse.

Two

December 30, 2009, two and a half years before I ran into that Amish buggy, Jose, the chaplain at Lutheran Hospital, was on the phone with my dad. But he wouldn't tell Dad anything specific about what had happened other than that I'd been in an accident. When Dad asked him if it was serious, Jose responded with, "Yes, Mr. Gerber, it's very serious." As my parents raced to Lutheran hospital, Mom had her hands on her head and her face buried between her knees, pleading with God for my life. As the chaplain's words sunk in, my dad tried to come to grips with the possibility that when he arrived at the hospital he might hear the news no parent wants to hear. His life might be about to change dramatically. Yes, in the span of just a few short years I was on both sides of the distracted-driving issue, first as the casualty and then as the cause.

When my parents arrived at the hospital they pulled right up to the ER entrance and rushed into the emergency room only to meet several staff members who had gathered at the desk area. After the nurses confirmed my parents' identity, my parents asked if I was alive. Not one staff member would answer that question directly. Instead, they merely replied that the doctor would talk to them soon. At that point the nurse asked the chaplain to take my parents to "the quiet room," which again led my dad to believe that the worst had indeed happened.

As they sat and again pleaded with God and waited for what seemed like forever, finally, one of the police officers entered the room to tell them a little about the accident. My mom pleaded with him while trying to contain herself. "Can you please tell us if he's alive?" In what was a dark time, they heard the officer say what they desperately wanted to hear: "Yes, he's alive, but he's in very serious condition." With that news they felt a ray of hope. They repeatedly thanked the Lord for sparing my life.

After a few more minutes passed, the doctor entered the room and laid out what was ahead. It was touch and go; he couldn't promise I'd survive. He said they could enter the emergency room and see me, but he warned them it could be very unsettling to see me hooked up to so many devices and so bruised and battered from the accident. Barely even hearing the doctor's words of caution, they ran down the hall, through the doors, and were immediately overcome with emotion as they saw the effects of the horrible accident.

My dad quickly came to my side and put his arms out over me and did what any God-fearing man would do; he prayed to the Great Physician, Jesus Christ, for healing, but ultimately for God's will to be done. My dad later said he has never had a more sincere prayer time than the twenty minutes spent next to my bedside. My mom continued to try to talk to me, sharing her love with me over and over again and reassuring me that everything would be okay. By that point Rachel and her mom arrived. They and my parents leaned on each other as fear and uncertainty reached new heights. Rachel was nauseated at the thought of what lay ahead for our young marriage. My family members called my grandparents and then started sending out texts to start a prayer chain. My dad was so overcome with emotion that he couldn't even talk to his dad, my grandfather. All he could manage to get out is that I'd been in a serious accident and they needed to come to Lutheran Hospital immediately. My grandpa responded solemnly: "We'll be right there."

Dad and Mom had always believed I was not their child but God's, and at that moment they prayed God would give them the strength and courage to trust Him if He did call me home for all eternity.

"We can't tell you much one way or the other right now. These next couple days will determine a lot. The brain is a complex part of the body, so every circumstance is a little different. We really have no idea at this point what he will be like a few days from now."

But before I tell you any more about the accident that nearly killed me, first let me give you another God story directly related to the accident: In December of 2009 I was working at Canterbury Schools in Fort Wayne. I was running an errand in a company truck and I was driving through a short section of road in a mall parking lot. I never wore my seat belt, and that day was no exception. I was going about thirty miles per hour, which was the speed limit, when suddenly I saw the flashing strobe lights behind me. I pulled over and got a $25 ticket for not wearing a seat belt. I was ticked. For the next couple weeks, though, I wore my seat belt. If I hadn't been stopped and ticketed a couple weeks before, I would not have been wearing my seat belt the day of that crash, and I wouldn't be here today to talk to others about what we've been through as a family. That was a God thing.

I called the Fort Wayne police station later, after I'd recovered, and spoke to the officer who had ticketed me months before. I told him how thankful I was that he'd given me a ticket that day for not wearing my seat belt. I told him I didn't know if he was a person of faith or not, but that I truly believed God had him in that place at that time to stop me and save my life a few weeks later. "It's not every day that we get calls thanking us for tickets we've given to people," the officer responded when I explained my situation to him. I assured him that if he had not spotted me that day, several weeks before I was hit, I would not have been alive to call and thank him!

So, back to the story of the accident: Let me fill you in on how all the details came together. On that sunny day, December 30, 2009, I had decided to take the day off from work because I had a doctor's appointment in the afternoon and a friend of mine was back from college for a few days and was going to stop by to catch up. It's weird how the brain works. I can remember spending a couple hours with Chase at my house like it was yesterday, but the rest of the day, and even events that happened the week or two before, are not in my memory bank. I was driving to that routine doctor's appointment in Fort Wayne when my life took that first dramatic turn. My wife and I had been married just six months, and already, at the tender age of twenty, she was facing the possibility of being a widow.

In hindsight, it's amazing to see how God was involved right from the start. One of the first few vehicles to arrive on the scene was driven by one of my bosses. He and his family had been visiting family in Bluffton and were on their way back to Fort Wayne. They'd never before taken the route they took that day, but for some reason they decided to switch things up that particular day. They drove up to the ac-cident scene, got out of

The other car slammed directly into me.

their vehicle, and began praying for whoever had been involved in the accident. Little did they know that they were praying for a guy they saw on a daily basis.

Police officers began trying to figure out how to contact my family to notify them of what had happened to me. They were able to identify me by plugging my informa-tion into the system at the hospital, since I'd been there before. The only person my file showed as being legally allowed to talk about my medical issues was my mom. Our old phone number was listed as the contact line, but had since been disconnected (who has landlines anymore, right). The back-up number was my parents' business number. Since this was around Christmas time, my parents had shut down their small business for the holiday season and were not at work. Fortunately, they had changed the answering machine message to include a cell number for my dad. The police reached my dad and told him they needed to talk with a Michelle Gerber. They definitely did some detective work to get the right person on the phone! They said it had taken about an hour from the time I arrived at the hospital to contact my mom.

Meanwhile, Rachel had just arrived home from work and was about to start cleaning the house. She sent me a text message while I was unconscious and at first didn't think much about me not responding. As time dragged on, though, she began to become concerned as to why I was not answering her texts or calls. She later told me that when my mom called her she started the conversation very normally. "Hey, Rachel, what are you up to today?" After some small talk, my mom tried her best to calmly tell her I'd been in an accident, but that she didn't have a lot of details.

Rachel then called her mother, who came over and drove her to the hospital, apparently faster than she normally drove. They both were hoping to be pulled over so that they could be escorted to the hospital by police after they explained what was going on. All the while Rachel was under the impression that I was either dead or dying. So when they arrived at the hospital and found three police officers stationed at the hospital entrance, and when one of those officers asked Rachel if she was related to Chandler Gerber, her first thought was that they were about to inform her of my death.

Three

I was still alive, but the medical staff people were not very forthcoming with answers for my family members. It wasn't that they were deliberately keeping things from my family; it was, as they eventually explained, that brain injuries such as the one I'd suffered are inherently complicated. Early on, they just couldn't be sure how things would turn out.

Over the next few days, things were touch and go. One hour my charts and numbers would be great, but the next hour my body would backslide. Hour after hour, people arrived to support my family and to pray for me. Meanwhile, my wife and my mother kept a journal of my

Traumatic Brain Injuries

"Traumatic brain injury (TBI) is a form of brain injury caused by sudden damage to the brain. Depending on the source of the trauma, TBIs can be either open or closed head injuries.

•Open Head Injuries: Also called penetrating Injuries, these injuries occur when an object (e.g., a bullet) enters the brain and causes damage to specific brain parts. Symptoms vary depending on the part of the brain that is damaged.

•Closed Head Injuries: These injuries result from a blow to the head (e.g., when the head strikes the windshield or dashboard struggles and my progress. Rachel sat up the entire first night, just staring at the monitor that charted my brain waves. Here are some portions of what Rachel wrote during those first few days and nights:

Accident reported at 12:59 p.m. at Baer Field Expressway and Lower Huntington Road. Mom and Dad got a call at 2:30 from Jose, the chaplain at Lutheran Hospital, saying to come right away, Chandler was in an accident, and it was very serious.

Mom and Dad arrived first and were not told much at all except that you were "alive right now." Later, the doctors told them that you were in an induced coma and on a ventilator.

Mom called me and told me what they

in a car accident). [I had a closed head injury.]

The Centers for Disease Control and Prevention reports that every year at least 1.7 million TBIs occur in the United States (across all age groups), and TBIs are a contributing factor in about a third (30.5%) of all injury-related deaths. Older adolescents ages 15 to 19 years, adults ages 65 years and older, and males across all age groups are most likely to sustain a TBI (Faul et al., 2010)."

http://www.asha.org/public/speech/disorders/TBI/

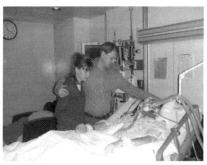

My parents prayed while I was in a coma.

knew, and we arrived at the hospital at 3:15. The doctor finally came and said they were going to take you into surgery to check the pressure on your brain and to check internally.

We got to see you and talk to you before the surgery. Then we all moved to the chapel around 4:00, and the family members began arriving as you went into surgery. …

Around 5:45 [the following day] *we were allowed to bring people back to see you, two at a time. Tons of people were here to support you, and prayer requests were being sent out like crazy. …*

The doctor then ordered a CT scan of your head to see what kind of swelling there was. … We were told that if there was going to be any more swelling, it would most likely happen in the next 48 hours. After that the swelling would hopefully go down slowly in the days to come. …

Saturday morning [two days after the accident] *they stopped your medicine and you opened your eyes a little. You didn't focus much, but they said that was to be expected.*

Sunday, January 3, was a great day because, according to Rachel's journal, when she kissed me I squeezed her hand "really hard." I'm sure she used the term "really hard" in a relative manner; I was too weak to squeeze really hard by most standards. I wish I could remember that moment though. But I also had a setback that day; I was having trouble breathing. An x-ray revealed that my left lung was collapsed. That meant going back on the ventilator.

Rachel wrote this the following day: *All day long you were pretty sedated, so we pretty much just left you alone. But around noon I went to check on you, and they said the neurologist was going to take out the probe in your head. They said your brain was healing well. You would need some rehab, but they weren't too worried about swelling.*

While I was in the coma over the following days, and as my numbers jumped up and down, someone suggested playing music in my room since I am a big music lover. My family figured that having some of my favorite songs playing softly in the background couldn't hurt anything. Around the time of the accident the Christian music group FFH (Far From Home) had released a new CD with one of the songs called "What it Feels Like." The lyrics to the chorus say the following: *"… and this may not be the road I would choose for me, but it still feels right somehow. 'Cause I have never felt you as close to me as I do right now. So this is what it feels like to be led."* Amazingly, the music actually did end up helping my numbers to stay in the "normal" range. The music played, and I heard it subconsciously.

I later talked with FFH front-man Jeromy Deibler, and when I told him those song lyrics spoke to me during my time of crisis and depression, he quietly said something about them being written during a trying time in his life, although I never got any details. Whenever those words were written and whatever circumstances surrounded the creation of the song, it became my personal theme song throughout the recovery process.

One of the things that added unneeded stress for my family was the fact that during the crisis I faced, no one doctor was in charge of the entire project. So, often, one of the doctors would recommend one thing, but a different doctor would disagree with the decision and recommend something else.

One of the worst things that happened was a day that they were trying to wake me up. My wife, mom, and mother-in-law were all around me trying to keep me calm as I was being brought out of the induced coma. I began struggling with the cords and wires attached to me, along with the tube down my throat, so the three of them began praying out loud as the doctors worked. They softly told me that Jesus Christ was with me and we would overcome. One of the doctors, who evidently was not a person of faith, became agitated with my family. She began yelling about how they were making things worse and how they needed to leave the room. Later, that same doctor talked with another doctor and told him my family was really causing problems. He too, became upset with the three ladies who were trying to calm me down. Finally, a third doctor, who actually had gotten along very well with my family, heard about what happened and threw the hammer down. The second doctor later apologized to my family, although they never did hear back from the initial trouble-making doctor. Complex situation, huh?

Despite the lack of physician coordination, on day eight, God performed what my family and I see as a miracle: I awoke from the coma and immediately recognized each of them. That was also the day the physical therapist helped me out of bed so I could sit in a chair. The following day more memories began to return. I was about to begin a long, hard road to recovery.

As I awoke from my coma and got to the point of starting to speak, my speech was very slow and at times hard to understand. My dad's first thought in hearing me speak was that there was definitely going to be some brain damage and that he was never going to have his son back as he knew me. Obviously my family had never been through anything like this and really did not know what to expect on a daily basis. My dad remembers going to the junk yard and seeing my car and just being in awe that I even survived the accident.

Because I still had so far to go in my recovery, someone was to stay with me round the clock, there in my hospital room. A few nights after I awoke from the coma, I awoke from regular sleep and needed to go to the bathroom. Seeing that Rachel, who was staying with me that night, had fallen asleep, I didn't want to wake her, so I chose to try to get to the bathroom on my own. As soon as I stood up I crumpled to the floor in a heap, which woke Rachel. She called for the nurses to come and help me. After all was settled from that calamity, she walked out into the hall and collapsed at the nurses' station, crying her eyes out. I wasn't the only one suffering; she was physically exhausted and emotionally drained.

Like my body, my mind wasn't functioning at a very high level at that point, either. At first I couldn't even talk, but I was able to write some things. At one point, feeling too warm, I wanted a fan to cool off. But I couldn't remember the word, so I wrote Rachel a note asking for a machine that blows to cool off.

When a therapist asked me to name the holiday in November when people eat turkey, I was at a loss. I also couldn't remember how to write a check. I couldn't walk at all for the first few days. But even so they sent me directly from ICU to begin rehab. I felt horrible, and my brain was still far from being fully recovered. The doctors had warned Rachel that my reduced brain functions might result in my having, at least at times, a surly attitude. They were right. During the early days of rehab and recovery I said some hurtful things to Rachel; I wish I could take them back.

As the weeks passed, struggling through various types of therapy became my routine. At about the one-month point, I was released from the hospital and allowed to do outpatient therapy. After a few more weeks, I began working a few hours a day, because, despite the crisis, the bills continued to arrive. Fortunately, my employers worked to find low energy jobs that I would be capable of handling, and for that I am very thankful.

I was overcoming the physical difficulties, but then doctors diagnosed me as having Post Traumatic Stress Disorder, which included depression and anxiety. Prior to this incident I'd never had any serious emotional health issues. But the anxiety attacks were debilitating. Each time one hit I felt as if my thoughts were moving at a thousand miles per hour, while everything else around me was moving in slow motion.

Worse yet, although I didn't recognize it at the time, the most difficult issue I faced was my anger toward the man who'd nearly killed me because he was too distracted to stop for a red light. The man didn't wake up that morning planning to slam into my car and nearly kill me, but something in me wanted to hate him anyway. The anger churned inside me, and part of me wanted to feed it, to indulge the bitter resentment.

I'd grown up in church. I knew what Jesus said about forgiveness. But knowing about forgiving was not the same as actually forgiving someone who nearly destroyed my life. I couldn't—or more likely, wouldn't—put into practice one of the basic tenets of the faith I'd long claimed to follow. Along with the depression and anxiety, this spiritual inconsistency was eating at me.

So, around the one-year anniversary of the accident, I wrote the man a letter, telling him I forgave him. Although the man never replied in any way, sending him that letter was a big step toward my emotional recovery. I felt a heavy emotional weight being released. I'd learned a very important lesson about forgiveness. Rachel and I resumed our lives. Eventually, everything continued as normal. Our future appeared to be bright—unspectacular, but good, happy, peaceful.

But I had more to learn.

Four

A lot can happen in two and a half years. But most of the events that occurred between my two tragedies were hard to even recall. Everything else paled compared to those pivotal events. My life was defined by two car crashes that dominated my thoughts.

Foremost in my thoughts following the second crash— my collision with the buggy—was anger at myself. How could I have failed to learn from the accident that had nearly killed me? If I had learned, those precious children would still be alive; that grieving family would still be together. *Please, Lord,* I pleaded in my thoughts, *let me really see how selfish it is to try to multi-task while driving. Please let me go back in time and really learn that lesson so that the second accident never occurs.*

But there was no going back. Time goes forward, exclusively. And I suspected I'd have a lot of time, almost certainly sitting in prison, to learn the lesson for real.

I began to sense that terrifying possibility, unmistakably, the day after the accident, when Officer Hernandez came to my parents' home, where Rachel and I were visiting. Had the officer not been so clearly compassionate, his size would have intimidated me. He started the conversation by asking what I remembered happening that morning. Again, I gave the same story, and I didn't leave out any details. I sensed God saying, "Okay, Chandler, I've given you a good life. You've served Me during the good times, but now will you serve Me during the bad times, or will you bend and sway?"

It's easy to tell those "little white lies" that we convince ourselves don't hurt anyone. Many people ask me why I didn't just throw my phone out into the field or not confess to texting while driving. I guess it's just so engrained in me to be honest that it didn't even cross my mind. I don't say that to brag; it's just the way it is. My whole life I'd been taught that honesty really is the best policy. Especially as I got older and became a Christian, honesty became a very important characteristic to me. After practicing honesty (or trying to) most of my life, it was just natural for me to tell the truth after I'd made a major mistake.

I asked Dio—Officer Hernandez told us we could address him by his first name—what I faced legally after truthfully disclosing everything I could remember about the accident. His candid reply sent chills through me: "You could face multiple felony charges since you were texting. Vehicular homicide, reckless homicide, vehicular manslaughter, and all on multiple counts due to the multiple fatalities."

My mind drifted to what life would be like locked up in federal prison. My wife was eight months pregnant with our first child. How would they make it financially? How would my daughter turn out if she grew up without her dad around? I snapped back to reality as Dio stood up and asked for my phone. I handed it to him, and he turned to leave. He paused, turned around, and asked a question I'll never forget: *"Would you guys be okay with me having a prayer with you before I go?"*

We were completely caught off guard because we'd never met this man before the accident, and we were busy dwelling on the possibilities he'd presented. "That would be great," I answered, surprise no doubt written across my face. We all stood in a circle in my parents' living room and held hands as Dio prayed for our family.

The last thing you expect in the midst of a criminal investigation is for the investigating officer to offer to pray for you and whatever you will be facing. Please don't misunderstand; he didn't pray for me to avoid punishment. He prayed that God would grant me and my family the grace to deal with whatever happened. When the prayer was finished, he left.

I'd started receiving hate-mail as well as messages of encouragement within hours of the accident, so I was in a really fragile state emotionally. Plus, I was seeing my name in newspapers, online articles, and television news reports. And, of course, loads of reporters were calling me, trying to get a comment. So Rachel and I decided to move in with my parents for a few days as we tried to sort out what had happened and what might happen as a result.

The following day, when I got up, my dad told me something I could scarcely believe. "Martin, the father of the family you crashed into, wants to meet with you and tell you he forgives you and that he's praying for you. He wants us to meet him at the hospital tonight."

A man who had lost two children the day before, had two family members in critical condition in the hospital currently, and who had every reason in the world to hate me, wanted to meet with me—to forgive me? We live in a small community, so news travels fast via the grapevine, which is how word got back to my dad about Martin's desire to meet with us. We talked about it as a family and decided it would be best to do whatever the Schwartz family wanted us to do, so we decided that night that we would meet with them.

My dad also said, "Chandler, do you remember what the banner on your phone said?"

"I couldn't tell you, Dad. That's the least of my concerns right now," I replied.

"You programmed your banner to say, "Use me, Lord." Well, He's using you, starting yesterday. Get ready."

Around that time, a song by Lecrae had been released. The song's chorus was, "Use me, Lord; use me, Lord; use me, Lord." It was really a cool thought, so I'd put it on my phone, thinking maybe God could use me to bring good in some way, somewhere. Little did I know that when you ask God to use you, you never know *how* He'll use you.

Before I could go up to the hospital to meet with Mr. Schwartz, I had to go meet with the attorneys who represented the insurance company. My boss and I thought it was a meeting to tell them what had happened and fill in some details. He picked me up and we drove, mostly silently, deep in thought, to Fort Wayne for the meeting. We continued downtown, found the building, and made our way to an elevator. We exited the elevator into a large office area. Two attorneys came out and escorted my boss into one room and me into a different room.

"We'll come and get you in a little while, Chandler," was all I was told.

So there I sat, thirty hours into this nightmare, stuck in an eight-by-ten interview room, waiting on these bigshot attorneys to call me in. Approximately an hour went by, and I was not doing very well. My boss and I thought we were going to be in the room together, simply recounting the accident. Instead, the attorneys separated us and kept me waiting for a long time, alone.

I'll never forget the look on my boss's face when they called me out and opened the door to the room he was in to let him out. He was stone-faced. I could tell that whatever they were going to be talking to me about was not going to be warm and fuzzy. They ushered me into another small office and shut the door. They were brutal. They didn't seem to care that my world was falling apart right in front of me. They shut that door and started telling me what I could and couldn't tell to which people. Actually, they told me I was to talk to no one except them about the accident from that moment on, period. When I mentioned that we were going up to the hospital that night to meet the Schwartz family, the attorneys threatened to drop the case if I didn't take their advice.

After being bullied for half an hour I finally threw my hands in the air and yelled, "Guys, stop it. Just stop it. There's one story; there's one version of what happened— the truth. I told it to the police at the scene of the accident; I told them the story at my parents' house, and I just told you. The story is not going to change. It's the same for everybody, so it doesn't matter who I tell it to."

One of the attorneys leaned back in his chair, grimaced, rolled his eyes, and mumbled, "Okay."

Then I said, "I'm tired, guys. We're done here; I'm leaving." With that, I got up and walked out, ending the meeting—and my relationship with them.

But perhaps those attorneys did make some impression on me. After talking it over with my family, we decided it would be best if I did not go see the Schwartz family at that point. But my parents and in-laws did go meet with them.

The following day, Dio, the investigating officer, called again and asked if I would be willing to give my testimony on the record. Having already told all the major players in the investigation the story, I said I would. My dad, my wife, and I drove over to the Adams County jail that afternoon and met with Dio. He told my wife and dad they could stay out in the parking lot while he recorded my interview and story of what happened.

The two of us walked down a long sidewalk to a back building, where Dio escorted me inside a small room. Keep in mind that this was somewhere around the forty-eight hour point since the accident, so the memories were all still incredibly raw. I walked in, Dio shut the door, and the interview began. He asked me to explain again what had happened; he would interject questions as needed.

I began talking, but after several minutes I just lost it; I couldn't stop crying. It was like a bad dream I couldn't wake up from. He spoke into a microphone and asked another officer to bring in some tissues as I tried to compose myself. We got through the interview, wrapped things up, and returned to my wife and dad. They asked how things were coming with the investigation, and we made some small talk. Dio then said something to us in the parking lot that I remember vividly: "I'd recommend you lawyer up. If I were you, I'd hire an attorney."

At that moment, it became very real that I could be facing time behind bars. It wasn't going to go away. As we walked toward our car I asked, "Well, now the question is, do we hire a lawyer, and if we do, who do we hire?"

Within seconds, my wife's phone beeped. It was a text from one of our closest friends. She worked for the prosecutor of a neighboring county, and he had heard about my situation and had some good defense attorneys in mind for me if I needed one. God was one step ahead of me on that one!

A couple days later we hired one of the best defense attorneys in Fort Wayne. Sadly, within that same timeframe, the oldest Schwartz son, Jerry, who had been airlifted to the hospital, passed away. My birthday is April 18th, so I had turned twenty-two the day after the accident. There I was, twenty-two years old, a child on the way, facing years and years behind bars, and I now had three fatalities on my conscience. My health started deteriorating. My world was collapsing around me.

Five

God didn't create humans to be alone. We all need people around us, to support, encourage, and keep us account-able or on track. When I look back at my life over the last several years, I see friends, family, and some mere acquain-tances, who stood by my wife and me during our setbacks. Another group who stood beside us was our church family. As followers of Jesus Christ, it's very important to have a support system of people around you, particularly a church family you can turn to in times of need. I am, and forever will be, grateful for my church, the Apostolic Christian Church. Many times people from the church visited the hospital in support of our family, visited the hospital in support of the Schwartz family, prayed for and visited us in our despair, and, just in general terms, loved us. The following is an example of the love and support our fam-ily has had over the last several years from members of our church body, friends in the community, and friends around the country. This is what my mother, Michelle, recalls from the 2009 accident:

When we had so many family and friends with us during Chandler's entire hospital stay, the nurses were amazed, and did not know what to do with everyone; we overtook the waiting room. That first night, they found a large conference room that was not in use and let us use that for probably five days, until it was needed for something else. It was such a blessing, because people came and stayed for long stretches of time, and also were bringing coolers of food and drinks for us. We never had to leave that room except to be in Chandler's room. It was so humbling to see the outpouring of love and support!

It was Christmas break from school, so Chandler's two brothers spent most of that time at the hospital. Their friends would come and sit with them, play cards, and talk. It was amazing to see teenagers giving up their Christmas break time so unselfishly! It really helped the boys with the passing of time and the stress of waiting to have their friends there. I think it was the second day that I got a text from a close friend. She told me that there was a prayer chain organized for around the clock that day and night. We had told people that Rachel and I had not slept the first night at all, and it was a long, difficult night. We received a text every hour all night long that second night from whoever was praying during that hour. Amazing! Such love! It truly was a blessing to know we were not alone. We were getting e-mails and text messages that there were literally people around the world praying for Chandler. It was really neat to hear how word can spread for the good!

When the doctors took Chandler off the ventilator the first time, it was a very trying day. He was not really awake or aware that day, and we just sat and talked to him so he would not be afraid. In the evening we noticed that he was taking shallow, quick breaths, and later that night they had to intubate him again. It was very disheartening and scary. One of his lungs had collapsed, and he could not breathe on his own. I believe he had to be on the vent maybe two more days before they tried again.

At that time, they began reducing the medicine that was keeping him unconscious. We had no idea what to expect. They had been telling us all along that the brain is a mystery, and there is so much doctors do not know about it. They had given *us different scenarios that could take place: he might have brain damage, might have a different personality, might have amnesia and not know any of us. Very scary!! That morning we were all in his room. It was a slow process. As he began to wake up, his eyes would twitch and flicker, but not open. At one point, he began cracking his knuckles, and we all stared at each other amazed. We told the doctor that he always did that, and they said that was a good sign. We just talked calmly to him, telling him where he was, that it was okay, and that we were there with him. Eventually he opened his eyes—very fuzzy looking, hard to focus. He could not speak because of the tube that had been down his throat. He would give us a thumbs up for a "yes" reply to our questions. He could not even smile or make expressions for a few days. It was kind of frightening, but the doctors told us that was normal because of the medication. I think it took maybe two days and then he could do a small smile. He had little lapses, even in rehab, but eventually most of his memory came back. He does not remember that Christmas or the day or so leading up the accident! We have shown him a lot of pictures so he can have a memory.*

I believe it was the day he was leaving the hospital to go to rehab—and he was extremely weak, and still foggy with memory lapses—that a nurse was making conversation with him about someone Chandler's age. I don't remember if it was a relative of hers, or what, but immediately Chandler said, "I know him! He was in my kindergarten class at school." We were all just amazed and started laughing, because we knew then that he had his memory! Definitely an "aha" moment!

Through this entire trial, we had so much love and prayers and support that it was absolutely incredible. One nurse actually asked at one point if we had someone famous there, because she had never seen so many visitors consistently for one patient! We absolutely could not have gone through this without the Lord and our loved ones. We commented so many times that we did not know how anyone that did not know Jesus personally could endure it!

I heard a story a few years back that addressed the need for Christians to have a local body of Christ to call their church family. The story goes like this: There was a man who said he was a Christian, but this man never attended church. "I don't have to be a church-goer in order to follow Jesus," he said. "I can stay home, read my Bible and pray, and everything will be fine." A friend of the man stopped by his home. It was a cold winter's day, so the man had a fire going in his wood-burning stove. The two men conversed for a while before the visiting friend cut to the chase. "We'd really like to see you in church this Sunday," he said kindly.

"I don't need to spend my Sundays at church! I can be a Christian without giving up a morning a week," the man replied.

The visitor slowly stood up, walked over toward the fire, and grabbed a metal fire-poker. Using the pole, he was able to move one of the red-hot coals at the bottom of the fire into isolation along the edge of the stove. In a matter of just a few minutes, the coal, as it stood alone, slowly began losing heat, and finally lost its color as the man who refused to attend church looked on.

Our Need for Others

"Ever console or scold people hurt in human relationships that satisfaction comes from God alone? Stop. Adam's fellowship with God was perfect, and God Himself declared Adam needed other humans."

John Ortberg Jr., *Everybody's Normal Till You Get to Know Them*

The visitor waved goodbye and walked out. He'd made his point. If we are continually away from believers in Jesus Christ, how can we expect to keep alive our fire for serving Him? The simple answer: We can't.

The point of that simple story is to illustrate the significance of having a group of people around you for support, especially other Christians. If you profess to being a Christian but don't regularly attend church, or for that matter never attend, I want to encourage you to seek out a strong, Bible-believing church to attend regularly and even become a member of. Seek out ways to serve your local church that you begin attending. Maybe Sunday school could use some help, or maybe there is another ministry there that could use a hand. Who knows, you could be just the person for the job!

Now with all that talk about "churches," let's establish what a "church" actually is. When I say the word "church" what picture comes to mind? A big, beautiful, elegant building with stained-glass mirrors and polished pews? Would it surprise you to know that in the book of Acts in the New Testament the "church" is never described as a building, but rather as a group of people? Obviously there is the worldwide church made up of all true Christians, but around the world, each area has its own local churches. In Acts 2:44-47, the "church" is described as a group of believers:

> All the believers were together and had everything in common. They sold property and possessions to give to anyone who had need. Every day they continued to meet together in the temple courts. They broke bread in their homes and ate together

with glad and sincere hearts, praising God and enjoying the favor of all the people. And the Lord added to their number daily those who were being saved.

They gathered in the temple courts, but that fact wasn't mentioned out of significance, but more as a location identifier. Over time, since the first century, probably out of a desire for organization more than anything, the believers began organizing into groups known as "churches." The bottom line is that if you are part of a church and your church building were to burn down tonight, you would still have a church tomorrow, because the people who worship together at that location are the church.

We may all have places we gather to worship corporately, but at the end of the day, we need to be sewn together not by what location we drive to on Sundays, but by a common faith in Jesus Christ, and by a loving relationship we

Church as Family

Here's a small sampling of the hundreds of well-wishes we got from our church family:

We are just pouring over you guys in prayer. I found an extra picture in my drawer of their [Rachel's and mine] engagement photos, and it's hanging on our fridge as a constant reminder.
–Andy & Jenna

So many are praying for Chandler's recovery. Your family is in our thoughts and prayers daily.
–Tim & Vicki

We are praying for you! We love you all.
–Eric, Steph, Karisa, Kylee

have with others who attend with us. Over the first few hours and days following my accident in 2009, attendees of our local assembly of believers were constantly in and out of the hospital, supporting me, my wife, and my family. When they left, they prayed for us night and day. Now I want to be that kind of support for others in need.

We have such a close-knit community here in the Midwest that friends and family who attend other churches were still there at the hospital to support us. That's what we need. We need more attendance at churches across the country so that the body of Christ will grow and strengthen, but we also need cooperation among the existing groups of believers. We saw a great coming together of different denominations during my first accident. The day of the accident in 2012, a minister from our local church stopped by and prayed with our family. He wasn't the only person to stop by. We had family, friends, and other people who traveled significant distances to stop by. Others sent messages or mailed cards of support.

Without that support, the emotional trauma would have been much more difficult to deal with. In addition to the support we received, the Schwartz family got a new buggy courtesy of the body of Christ is this area. They had help sorting out medical bills and paperwork courtesy of the body of Christ too. It was really incredible to watch. Trauma struck, and the "church" went into action.

I felt truly blessed, but I still faced some dark times….

Six

I poured out my heart in a journal during those dark days:

I'm sorry, Lord. Please forgive me. Please forgive me for crashing into an Amish family and killing two of their children. I didn't mean to do that, Lord, and I wish I could go back and change what happened that day. I don't know why it happened, Lord. I don't know why two children died and I'm not physically injured from the crash. I don't know why these things keep happening to me, Lord. I don't know how strong You think I am, but You have pushed me farther than I ever would have thought was possible for me to handle. I don't know.

That seems to be my response to a lot of the things that happen in life. I don't know. I don't know why I had to be driving on that road at the time I was. And I don't know why they had to be driving on that road at the same time. I can't understand. I don't understand why two children had to die that day. I don't understand why two families had to be changed forever, the Amish family and my family. They lost two children that day, and I will forever have the images of what I saw that day and the reality of what happened to haunt me. Lord, I know that You say in the Bible, "All things work together for good for those who love God." I'm trying to understand that.

I'm trying to understand what good will come from this. I'm trying to understand what I can do to bring beauty from the ashes. I'm trying to figure out where to go from here. I keep thinking about what would be going through my mind if someone hit and killed my two brothers. I would be crushed. I would be mad and sad and confused all at the same time. It's only by Your grace that people get through these things.

It's only by Your grace that a guy at 22, with a young wife and a baby on the way, can get through these things.

I think about my dad losing his mom to cancer when he was in high school, and I never have been able to understand how he could get through that. I think of Jim and Jenny losing their daughter in a car crash years ago, and I had never before been able to relate to that kind of pain. Now I can. Now I understand how they could get through that. It's with You.

I think of the poem my mom had hanging in our house when I was growing up. The poem was called "Footprints in the Sand." It talks about a man looking back at the footprints in his life, showing all the times he'd been walking through events. There are two sets of

Why does God allow suffering?

"The church has a history of formulizing suffering, giving it tidy origins and endings and whitewashing the horrid, debilitating middle. We've assessed the complicated nuances of universal sorrow and assigned it categories, roots, principles. Or in the face of uncertain causes, we recite some of the coldest, inhumane theology: 'God is sovereign. Deal with it.' In an attempt to understand the ordinary grief of human life, I fear we've reduced a complicated reality to an unmanageable burden; we've put a yoke of despair on people who mourn, assigning accolades to those who 'suffer well' and, in ways overt and subtle, urging our *footprints. The man's foot-prints and Jesus' foot prints. As the man is looking back, he notices that at the most dif-ficult points in his life there was only one set of footprints. He asks Jesus why He left him during those low points. Jesus just smiles and tells him, "It was during those low points that I carried you. Those are My footprints." Growing up, I could never relate to that. Low points? My low points*

brokenhearted to buck up. Then adding insult to injury, we fall into the trap of ex-plaining suffering, as if any one of us could possibly un-derstand its eternal scope."

Jen Hatmaker, quoted in "Why Does God Allow Pain and Suffering?" http://www.crosswalk. com/blogs/christian-trends/why-does-god-allow-pain-and-suffering.html

were days when we were out of my favorite cereal, or days when my friends couldn't come over. Now? Yeah, I can relate. Now my low days are when I crash into a family and kill two of their children. Yeah, I can relate to that poem now.

I just opened the Bible and turned to the book of Job. I read the first couple chapters where Job goes from being a highly suc-cessful and blessed man, to a point of complete despair. He loses children, and animals, and possessions in a matter of moments. At the end of chapter two, Job's wife says, "Are you still holding onto your integrity? Curse God and die!" Job then said something in a way that I had never thought of before. Job said to his wife, "You are talking like a foolish woman. Shall we accept good from God and not trouble?"

Life has been pretty good for me during my first 22 years here in America. Should I keep asking for all the blessings without expecting any of the pain? Obviously nobody goes looking for needless pain. I just keep thinking of the process of refining gold.

It takes fire, intense fire. I would say that right now I'm going through some intense fire, and so is my family. I look around and I see other people who are currently going through trials too, or I see people who have gone through trials before. I know this is a big world and I'm not the only human being with problems. I know there are people with much bigger problems. People I know personally have terminal cancer. People I know personally have other terminal diseases.

Even so, at the time, I felt that in my relatively few years of life I'd already dealt with more than my share of trials. When I was in my teens, for a year or two I had a pain in my groin, but I did my best to ignore it. When I finally went to the doctor he said I had a hernia that needed to be repaired with surgery. At fifteen years old I went under the knife for the first time. It was not a big deal in hindsight, but at the time it really seemed like a huge deal for me! *What if I don't wake up from the anesthesia?* I pondered. The night before the surgery, with me being the oldest of three sons, and with none of us ever having undergone surgery before, my parents called us all into the den of our house and we all knelt and prayed. My dad got a little choked up, which in turn caused me to choke up, and the next thing you know it was even more emotional! Funny now, scary then. It all went fine, though, and life moved on.

A few years later I'd been noticing for a while that food kept getting stuck in my chest after I swallowed. I didn't think much of it until finally I could hardly eat without the fear of suffocating to death. The episode that convinced me to go see a doctor was when I was leaving my cousins' house after eating a piece of pizza, as I walked toward the car. I began to panic as the food lodged in my esophagus. Finally, after several minutes of making weird faces, grimacing, and moving all around, I was able to get the food to go down.

I went to the doctor, where I learned that I had a rare esophagus disease known as Achalasia. My esophagus was basically paralyzed, so I needed to have another surgery at Riley Children's Hospital in Indianapolis. The average person's esophagus flexes when they swallow, allowing the food or drink to easily pass into the stomach. My esophagus stays completely still, which causes food to lodge in my chest, leaving me feeling as if I'm going to choke or that I can't breathe. It was very humbling to be eighteen years old and getting a major operation done at a children's hospital. But, apparently, at the age of eighteen you can go either way, and the surgeon who could best serve me was a pediatric surgeon. Walking in to the hospital that morning was really awkward as I passed toddlers and little children.

When I woke up from surgery at the hospital I was in intense pain. For the next month I had horrible experiences trying to eat again. As my esophagus was trying to heal from surgery, the swelling caused continued problems. The doctors told me not drink any carbonated beverages for the rest of my life, so as to not complicate the Achalasia. I was warned that my throat would feel weird sporadically, and that I wouldn't be able to belch, hence the no-carbonation rule. But, again, God gave me the grace to get through, and to this day and for the rest of my life, I will continue to deal with Achalasia.

A little more than a year after learning to live with Achalasia came the first accident, the one in which I was nearly killed. Then, stress, brought on by anxiety attacks resulting from the crash, caused my esophagus to spasm, which was incredibly painful, and which caused still more stress —a horrible cycle. And that continued for a while, until eventually God relieved me of the situation I was in and, through the appropriate levels of medication and continued therapy, removed the anxiety attacks from my life.

But then, two years after that, came the very worst day of my life, April 17, 2012. This was my journal entry one week after that day:

When I was one day away from turning twenty-two years old, my whole world froze. I remember the day well. It's been a week ago at this point, but I want to write this all down so my kids, grandkids, and great grandkids can read this someday and realize that God can bring us through anything.

I remember waking up knowing that Shawn and I would be doing a project at work together that day in New Haven. We normally worked in separate areas of the business. Resource Maintenance, a carpet cleaning and janitorial supply business, is owned by Rachel's uncle, Shawn's dad. Shawn and I were heading to a large commercial job that day. He had to put fuel in another vehicle he was driving so he told me to head to the job and he would meet up with me there, or on the way if he could catch up.

I remember pulling off of Wabash Street in Bluffton, and turning left on Main Street. Then I turned right onto U.S. 124, which I was going to follow for ten or fifteen minutes before my next turn. The sun was blinding; it was just rising and I was driving straight east, right into the glare. I remember putting the sun visor down and trying to shield my eyes so that I could see. I could only see a few feet in front of the van, but I knew we had to get to the job on time, so I kept driving.

The night before, Rachel and I had been talking about a house that we were considering buying for a rental, so I decided to text her. I just asked her if she wanted to wait until Shiloh was born to do anything with any houses. She said yes, and that we could talk about it when we both got home that night. Another message or two were sent back and forth, and at some point around then my life hit its lowest. It seemed like everything was in slow motion. I was driving along between 55 and 60 miles per hour, and I could hardly see because of the sun. On top of that, Rachel and I had been texting each other as I was driving. Then it happened. BOOM!

Just when it seemed that things were really looking up after my recovery from the first accident, our entire life was turned upside-down again: people were dead because of my carelessness! And while the first accident, when I was the victim, had brought Rachel and me closer together and strengthened our faith, this accident, which I caused, threatened to pull us apart and was challenging our faith. I'm afraid to think what might have happened during those dark days had it not been for the prayers and support from family and friends.

Rachel later confided in me that although the first accident had made our relationship stronger, the second time around, when I was responsible, she felt more distant from me for a while. Honestly, I can't blame her. I'd dragged her along behind me through two major incidents. She innocently stood by and was sucked into the crazy mess that I called life. She's always been so supportive and loving through everything we've dealt with, but she told me that she really was kind of irritated with me after the second accident. *I didn't do anything. Why can't I just live a normal life?* Those were the thoughts of my innocent twenty-two-year-old wife after handling a lifetime volume of major trials in just two years. I thank God for her!

Seven

I continued to journal as the wait dragged on:

April 26, 2012

Well, it's 2:45 in the afternoon. Rachel and I just took Adler, my nephew, out to eat for lunch at McDonald's for his fourth birthday, which was yesterday. Now Rachel is at a doctor's appointment and then she's going to babysit Jeremy and Sarah's girls for a couple hours. I kept thinking throughout the hour or so that we spent with Adler about how innocent he seemed and how oblivious to all my problems he was.

Sometimes I wish I could go back in time to when I was four or five. Life would be easier. I could sleep in at my parents' house and wake up without a care in the world. No bills to pay, no responsibilities. I would just be with my brothers and parents, and all my needs would be met. I could go out in the yard and run around and play and go inside and eat breakfast, lunch, and supper.

The innocence of children is the mindset we need to take on spiritually as adults. Jesus said in Matthew 19:14, "Let the little children come to me, and do not hinder them, for the kingdom of heaven belongs to such as these."

We need to realize that we do not need to overthink things in life. My car accidents and life experiences thus far have really shown me that. When I was lying in a hospital bed for two weeks after my first car accident, the last thing on my mind was making more money, or wondering what job God would have me doing in five years. I was reading the Bible and reading about what Jesus wanted me to live like. I was thinking about how I could influence people for Christ through the whole event.

It's been times like those in my life that I really realize what is important. Even now, as I'm writing, I keep thinking about Adler eating his chicken nuggets, and his Oreo ice cream afterwards. He was so happy to have the basics of life. He didn't need a five-star restaurant to be happy. A simple McDonald's happy meal made him smile. I just kept listening to him babble on as he ate, and I just kept thinking about my life when I was growing up.

But now that I'm home and alone, thinking and writing and praying, I think about my own daughter who is going to be here, God willing, in a month. I feel so excited to meet her, and yet

Dangers of holding on to anger

"New research suggests constant bitterness can make a person ill.

In the study, Concordia University researchers examined the relationship between failure, bitterness and quality of life.

'Persistent bitterness may result in global feelings of anger and hostility that, when strong enough, could affect a person's physical health," said psychologist Dr. Carsten Wrosch. ...

Wrosch and co-author Jesse Renaud, a doctoral student, single out failure as one of the most frequent causes of bitterness. Feelings of anger and accusation are often found with bitterness.

Unlike regret, which is about self-blame and a case of 'woulda, coulda, shoulda,' acrimony points

I feel so much responsibility. God is going to use me to be her earthly father, and to raise her up knowing about Jesus.

Another thing God is teaching me through this second car accident is love. I've never been a patient person. I'm often judgmental, short-tempered, critical, and irritable toward people who are around me. I know I should not be like that, and so for years I half-heartedly worked on improving those areas of my life. Then, after my first car accident, I grew so much spiritually that it's a night-and-day difference when I think about pre-accident Chandler versus post-accident Chandler.

the finger elsewhere—laying the blame for failure on external causes.

'When harbored for a long time,' Wrosch said, 'bitterness may forecast patterns of biological dysregulation (a physiological impairment that can affect metabolism, immune response or organ function) and physical disease.'"

http://psychcentral.com/news/2011/08/10/bitterness-can-make-you-sick/28503.html

But even having grown so much spiritually in the weeks and months following that accident, often I still was short-tempered and critical of people. But after this second accident, which was my fault, I really have seen true love. I've heard from many people who have been up to see the family that lost two children and that still has two members in the hospital, one of whom we are not sure is going to make it, and they are completely forgiving toward me; they are completely letting go of any and all hostility toward me.

Within the last few days I read in 1 Corinthians 13:4-7, where Paul says, "Love is patient, love is kind. It does not envy, it does not boast, it is not proud. It is not rude, it is not self-seeking, it is not easily angered, it keeps no record of wrongs. Love does not delight in evil but rejoices with the truth. It always protects, always trusts, always hopes, always perseveres." That describes the kind of love that we as Christians should have, and that describes the kind of love the Martin Schwartz family has shown me, without ever having met me since the accident. It is humbling.

Ever since April 17, 2012, God has given me the realization that, as a follower of Christ, I need to show that level of love. Suddenly, things that used to tick me off no longer bother me. Suddenly, people who used to make me really mad no longer frustrate me.

My first job out of high school was working maintenance at a private school in the area. I had worked over the summers while I was in high school, and then had been hired on full time after graduation. The environment that I worked in was different from the environment I lived in outside of work, to say the least. Crude language, crude jokes, and disrespectful treatment were the daily norm for me as I worked there. After

Prayer to Release Anger

Heavenly Father,

Please help me to dwell on the good and the positive in my life. I know that it is You who examines our hearts. Search the inner depths of my heart and expose anything that is not of You so I can be set free of it.

Lord, where I have directed anger toward others in my life or held anger inside of me, I confess that as sin and ask You to forgive me and take all the anger away. Heal any wounds that I have inflicted, through my words and actions, in others and myself. Help me to speak sweet words and healing, for I know that pleases You. Where I have shown anger toward others I confess it to you as sin. Bring Your restoration to every situation where it is needed.

Thank You, Lord, that You will redeem my soul in peace from the battle that *three summers of part-time work, and two years of full-time work, I parted ways with the organization. Up until the time of my accident, from time to time I would still feel bitterness and anger flashing through my mind when memories would come up of that job. I would think about times my boss or one of the older guys had mocked me or called me stupid, and my blood would boil. I thought about all the times I'd been mistreated and I wanted to scream!*

No more. No more anger from me toward them. I took the lives of two of Martin Schwartz's children in a car

is against me. I believe that You, the God of peace will crush the enemy under my feet. Help me to live righteously because I know there is a connection between obedience to Your ways and peace. Help me to depart from thoughts of anger and bouts with depression; help me to seek peace and actively pursue it. Thank You that You will take away all anger in me and keep me in perfect peace, because my mind is fixed on You Father. In Jesus' name I pray. Amen.

http://revivedlife.com/prayer-to-release-anger/

accident, and he has forgiven me—immediately, and with no reservations. I impacted his family in a way that I doubt he ever thought they would be affected, and yet he has shown me love. How can I hold on to anger and bitterness from memories of high school or my first job when Martin isn't holding on to anger after losing two children? I can't. God has used Martin Schwartz and his family to teach me what love really is. "Love is patient, love is kind ... it is not easily angered, it keeps no record of wrongs." I don't know if anyone will ever read this down the road, but if you are reading, please, please, please, release any anger you're hanging onto. Let it go.

Eight

Love is patient, but, sadly, patience has never been my greatest strength. I hate waiting in line at a checkout counter or a restaurant; I hate waiting for the flu to work its way out of my system; and I especially hated waking up every day, wondering, "Will today be the day?" I was waiting for a call from my defense attorney letting me know whether or not I was going to be charged. It was like my whole life was hanging in the balance every moment of every day. I'd been told at one point that I'd be able to turn myself in rather than have police cars haul me away. I found little comfort in that.

Actually, being patient still is difficult for me. Sometimes I wonder if I'm the only one who feels that I just can't make any progress. I'm talking about specific areas, like, in my case, becoming more patient. Maybe you think back to high school and an issue you had in your life, and now, five years later, it's still an issue; you can't seem to let it go. There are a few things in my life, some spiritual and others emotional and physical, that I just can't seem to shake.

I recently heard about a well-known and very popular singer songwriter from the 90s. He told his record producers, right from the start, that he never wanted to know how many CDs he sold or how much money he was actually worth. He drew an average salary and gave the rest away, without ever even knowing how much he was giving away. It's said that he was a millionaire, but you never would have known it, because he was such a humble guy. Sounds like a great story, right? Well, the problem was that he was an alcoholic. This guy was out there making music to glorify God, giving his money away to stay humble, and making a huge difference for the cause of Christ, but he couldn't put the bottle away after growing up in an abusive household.

I'd say that that man is in the presence of God today because he seemed to have trusted Jesus' payments for his sins, and fought against that hold in his life and strove to draw others to Christ. Meanwhile, I'll never forget a conversation I had with a man a year ago. He flat out told me he believes that if a person cannot overcome an issue in his or her life, then that person is hiding sin from God and not repenting of certain things. He said that if that person truly repented, then God would free him. I was shocked. Obviously that's ridiculous.

If the musician from the story above was being a great example to the world, but he had an issue in his life that was his "thorn in the flesh," that doesn't mean he wasn't a follower of Christ. It just meant that the devil had a hold on an area of his life. I can understand. If we're honest, I think we all can relate, whether it's gossip, smoking, lust, or you fill in the blank. Only Jesus lived a perfect life. If we were perfect, we wouldn't need Jesus.

Lately I've thought a lot about Paul's admonition to avoid having even a hint of (you name the sin) in your life (see Ephesians 5:3), and I've come to the conclusion that we need to be continually striving to "not have a hint of ____" in our lives, but none of us is there yet. I've heard before that the Christian life is a journey, not an arrival at a destination upon acceptance of Christ. All Christians are working toward being more like Christ. We're all pushing against the things of this world as followers of Jesus. It's not easy. Anyone who says that being a Christian is easy is either lying or hasn't been a Christian for more than twenty-four hours.

Christ called for His followers to deny our flesh, to deny the very character that was sown into each of us from birth in this fallen world. Jesus said that whoever would follow Him should take up his cross daily. As Christians, we're supposed to pick up our cross and daily fight against our addictions, our sins, and our shameful desires as we follow after Christ. But neither Jesus nor any of His disciples said doing so would be easy. If anyone has a Staple's easy button for the Christian life, let me know because I'd love to tap that button virtually every day! I'll leave it with this paraphrased verse from the Bible: "The things that are seen are temporal, but the things that are unseen are eternal."

But anyway, getting back to my story, life moved on. The days turned into weeks, and the weeks turned into months, and still no call with any information. I began preparing for the worst as we moved our family across town to a better neighborhood because I wanted my wife and daughter to be safer if I had to be gone a long time.

Here's my journal entry from right around that time:

A few days ago, Friday morning, the police notified my dad that they were done with the investigation and had turned all the information over to the prosecutor. I felt panic welling up inside me all day as I kept thinking about what could happen. My wife is nine months pregnant and due tomorrow. On the other hand, I'm waiting to hear what will happen with my life's course. So much stress has been building up inside me. For some reason, on Friday, the same day I found out that the prosecutor now has the information, Verizon phones were down all afternoon and evening.

I remember very well that day the phones were down. I was at work in the afternoon and suddenly I could receive calls on my phone, but I couldn't answer them. I could see who was calling, but I didn't have the signal strength to be able to answer the call. I had several calls from my wife and a couple voicemails were left, although I couldn't listen to those either. My stomach began to hurt. I kept wondering, while I was working, if something was wrong. Our baby was due and we were waiting to hear from the prosecutor, so I began to sweat as I wondered if Rachel had heard something that I hadn't.

I quickly left work, put all my supplies down, and ran to my car to drive home. A few minutes later I pulled up to our house and saw Rachel pulling her car out of our garage. When she saw me drive up she jumped out of the car and began sobbing as she said, "Where have you been? I've been trying to call you!" After a minute or two we realized that nothing major had happened; Rachel had just wanted to ask me a question. But when she couldn't reach me, she began panicking. With each missed call and voicemail, I began panicking more, too. After we figured out that the whole thing was one big misunderstanding, my chest began to hurt. I thought, *Please, God, don't let me have a heart attack! Not now!* I really felt as if I couldn't make it one more day.

Even the phone system seemed to be against me, I thought—briefly, before reminding myself again that God is in control.

Each day that I drove a van for work, I vividly remembered that horrible day. The image of the bodies lying around the smashed buggy still haunted me. Every night I was called in to work late I was filled with regret over the time missed with my family. So I changed jobs to something less time-consuming and with more straight-forward hours because I couldn't handle continuing on with the company I was with when I caused the accident. With too many horrible memories and deep regrets, we parted ways.

Every few weeks it seemed that some news reporter would run a story about the continuing deliberation by the county prosecutor, and that would stir things up. I would then get calls from several other reporters looking for my comments or thoughts, but I always declined to say anything.

Just before the one-year anniversary of the accident, my attorney called me: "The prosecutor has decided to put the decision of whether or not to charge you to a grand jury, Chandler. Starting Monday, they will begin selecting jurors, and then the group will decide." I can still hear those words. The prosecutor was really in a tough spot. He was an elected official, and some people wanted him to make an example of me, while others, including the Amish within the community, wanted to drop all charges and move on. Any decision the prosecutor made, he knew he was going to upset people.

Over the course of a week or so, the jurors heard my video testimony, saw my written testimony, heard from people who were first at the scene, and were shown all kinds of information to give them details into every aspect of the crash.

It all came down to a Friday, just a little more than a week before Easter. My attorney told me the jury had reviewed all the details, heard all the testimonies, and they were going to make an announcement by Friday afternoon. What a miserable week, and what a horrible day Friday was. Every time my phone rang I got a little sick to my stomach. I worked that Friday morning and into the early afternoon. I got home and just waited out the last few hours. Those hours passed, and still no call. I'd been preparing all week for that day. Emotionally, I was as ready as I ever could be for the news that I'd face a long, hard trial.

I was told I'd have an answer one way or the other by Friday at five. Five came and went, and still nothing. I was on my bed on a sunny April afternoon, around five-thirty, just crying and telling God I couldn't go through another day like that. "God, I've lived in constant fear for a year," I prayed. "Why couldn't they just give me an answer one way or the other, today?" As I lay there, feeling sorry for myself again, I remembered that my mom had texted me something earlier in the day. I grabbed my phone and scrolled through a few texts until I found what she'd sent.

"Hey, bud," the text read. "I was doing devotions this morning and I read Psalm 91. If you get a chance today, you should read it!" I hadn't thought much of the text earlier in the day as I was working and my adrenaline was sky high, but at that moment, while I was sobbing in my bed, I grabbed my Bible.

Psalm 91 starts like this: "He who dwells in the shelter of the Most High will rest in the shadow of the Almighty. I will say of the LORD, 'He is my refuge and my fortress, my God, in whom I trust.'" As I read those words, a peace began creeping into my heart and soul. I continued reading, and when I got to verses fourteen and fifteen, I felt that God was telling me things were going to be fine, if I trusted in Him. "'Because he loves me,' says the LORD, 'I will rescue him; I will protect him, for he acknowledges my name. He will call upon me, and I will answer him; I will be with him in trouble, I will deliver him and honor him....'"

I sat up in bed and thought to myself, "What am I doing? Get out of bed, you big baby! You have God the Father who will take care of you, whether you are in prison or not." I read those last few verses so many times I lost count. I inserted my name whenever it read "he" or "him." It made it really personal, like God actually was talking to me. I got out of bed and lived the rest of the night like a new man.

I sat there reading through the book of Psalms and I came across gems like these: "Test me, LORD, and try me, examine my heart and my mind; for I have always been mindful of your unfailing love and have lived in reliance on your faithfulness.... Guard my life and rescue me; do not let me be put to shame, for I take refuge in you.... For the sake of your name, LORD, forgive my iniquity, though it is great.... The LORD is my light and my salvation—whom shall I fear? The LORD is the stronghold of my life—of whom shall I be afraid...." Verse after verse, chapter after chapter, of so much encouragement that the Lord is good! I don't know what you are dealing with today, but I've been at the bottom. I've had hard times. The Lord is good. Don't give up.

My wife has had it on her heart for a while that we needed to be helping kids in some way. I'd felt that way too, for a few years. We sponsor a few kids through various charities and organizations, but we sensed that God was calling us to something else. We just don't know what that something else is. Isn't that how God works, though?

It seems like He always gives His people circumstances or a sense of needing to do something, but He won't make it easy on us and show us exactly how it's supposed to play out. He leaves that up to us. We're supposed to figure it out. So many times I wish I could literally ask God to His face what He wants me to do and hear His specific, detailed answer, but that's obviously not reality. Although it would make being a Christian easier!

Some Mormons or Jehovah's Witnesses came to our house a few years back, and I finally answered the door after years of dodging them. They asked me if I believed in modern-day prophets. It kind of caught me off guard at first, but I thought about it for a second, and then I told them no. I told them that in Old Testament times, God used prophets to relay His messages to the people. In New Testament times His Son Jesus was here and gave us an example. In the post-ascension world, after Jesus left the earth, His disciples gave us more examples. Now we live by faith, guided by His Word, the Bible. I guess that's why God doesn't just give us direct answers to our questions in life; we live by faith, not by sight.

If God told us the answer to every question we had, we'd have no need for faith. The apostle Thomas didn't believe that Jesus had come back to life, and when Jesus finally appeared to Thomas He told the skeptical apostle that he believed because he saw, but blessed are those who do not see yet believe. That's where we all are. It's tough for me to read stories online and watch the news. I worry about my kids and about what life will be like in the future.

I guess I'm like Thomas. Jesus said not to worry about tomorrow, for each day has enough problems of its own. I'm constantly wondering about what to do financially or what to do about school for our kids in a few years, and things like that. Maybe I just need to believe that Jesus will work everything out and not get stressed about the details. I can't see Jesus, but I know He's here. I haven't seen God, but He has directed my life. Our sense that God was calling us to help kids has been answered in a way we never would have imagined. We're making teenagers aware of the dangers of distracted driving. We never could have imagined that scenario being the way God would give us for reaching kids.

Anyway, the next morning after my meltdown and reassurance from Psalms, just a little more than two weeks before the one-year anniversary of the accident, we had a family Easter. My wife's uncle Jeff, who had been my employer at the time of the accident, was there. I was in better spirits than the day before, but I was still not enthusiastic.

"Hey, Chan! Did you get any news?"

"No, I didn't hear anything," I replied. A few minutes passed and Jeff motioned me over to the side of the room where Shawn was standing.

"Chan, we thought you knew. We ran into the prosecutor last night at the high school carnival and he told us that the grand jury decided to drop all charges. He couldn't get a hold of your attorney, so he was going to try again Monday. You're free! It's all over."

My whole world stood still as I heard those words. I was overjoyed, excited, and thankful. Everybody at the gathering was giving me hugs and telling me how happy they were for our family. I ran outside and called my parents, and my mom started crying. It was one of the most incredible feelings I've ever had to know that my life wouldn't be spent behind prison bars. I'd get to be a father to my new daughter!

Nine

Over the next few days, months, and years I received messages on Facebook, some positive and affirming, and others not so nice. I'll never forget a hate message I got from some guy in Canada. I can't remember all the details of the message, because I promptly deleted it, but it started something like this: "I hope you read this message all the way through. I just saw your commercial and I decided to write you. You are an awful person who in my mind is worse than a child molester. You should be in jail for the rest of your life, and I hope you rot in hell. You are not welcome in my country...." I sat there in disbelief.

I've never responded to any hate mail—until I got that message. Before I deleted it, I couldn't contain myself. I replied with something to the effect of, "Good thing you opinion doesn't matter to anyone. God bless you, have a nice day." I should not have written that in reply, but I honestly couldn't believe that someone would take time out of their day to write to someone they don't even know to spout off about something they know nothing about.

Others, using fake screen names, threatened to kill me or do other terrible things to me to make me pay for my mistake. I guess my wife and other family members were right in telling me not to read them, but I felt compelled to do so—I'm not sure why. After those first few days, though, my wife and I remembered the commitment we'd made while we were waiting, eight months earlier. Our slogan as a family had become "Beauty from Ashes." We were determined to bring good from bad. We thought that meant going to a couple local schools, or maybe talking in a Sunday school class or two. Little did we know that our story was just getting started.

I spent a few weeks making phone calls to hospitals, schools, and organizations that were campaigning against distracted driving, but I couldn't get a single call or email returned. I made repeated calls back to the same places I'd called the first time, thinking that maybe they just forgot to get back to me, but they never replied. Then one evening, as I arrived home from work, my phone rang, and when I looked at the screen it showed a California number.

It has to be either a misdial or somebody who just moved to the area, I assumed. I picked up, though, and the person on the other end of the line was no one I would have expected.

"Hey, Chandler, my name is Theresa and I work with Werner Herzog here in Los Angeles. I'm a researcher for his documentary and film projects. Werner has been hired by AT&T, Verizon, Sprint, and T-Mobile to put together a powerful documentary discouraging texting and driving. We've been trying to get a hold of you since the charges were dropped against you to see if you would be interested in being a part of the film." I couldn't believe what I was hearing. A famous Hollywood director had been trying to contact me?

Theresa continued, "The film will feature four different texting and driving stories, showing the dangers from victims' views as well as from those who caused the disasters. It will be put on YouTube and NetFlix and distributed to forty-thousand public high schools around the country. Would you be interested in being involved?"

I asked a few questions, and then asked for a little time to talk with my wife. I hung up the phone and glanced up to the sky, thanking God for opening a door for me. As Rachel and I talked about the call and offer that I'd just received, we knew it was God's way of adding momentum to our whole "Beauty from Ashes" idea. We thought we might impact some people around our town, but God had much bigger plans.

I called Theresa back a little later that evening and told her we'd love to be involved. She told me that in a couple weeks they'd fly out to Indiana to film my portion of the documentary. I hung up the phone that night with my head spinning.

The prophet Jeremiah wrote the following lines in his Old Testament book of the Bible: "'For I know the plans I have for you,' declares the LORD, 'plans to prosper you and not to harm you, plans to give you hope and a future.'" It can be debated what exactly Jeremiah was talking about or who he was speaking to, but if you pull it out of context, it's one of the more encouraging verses in Scripture. We learned that night that the prophet Isaiah was right when he wrote by the power of the Holy Spirit, "'For my thoughts are not your thoughts, neither are your ways my ways,' declares the LORD." Looking back from that point to the year before, we realized how far we'd come and how God was starting to show us His plan for our lives. A year before, I couldn't understand why I was going through the things I'd faced. Then, a year later, God was revealing how He was going to use my tragedies to encourage others.

About that time, we were trying to make arrangements for me to go meet the Schwartz family. I wanted to apologize to them and let them know how incredibly sorry I was. I was committed to raising awareness and doing everything I could to redeem the tragedy. Looking back, I realize now the real power of forgiveness. I've held off until now to copy the letter I received from Martin, the father, just a couple months after the accident. Keep in mind, this man had just had his oldest son, his little girl, and his little boy killed in a crash that I'd caused a few short months before he wrote this letter to me. What follows is, nearly verbatim, the copy of the letter I'm holding in my hand right now.

Trusting in Gods ways. How does this find you? Hope all in good health and in good cheer. Around here we are all on the go and try to make the best we can. My Son Michael is working on a crew he like very much Jacob is working for Dean Gerber with hogs vacc. power washing. Today is such a beautiful day a nice cool breeze such a blessing a little on the dry side but God will sent us rain when we deserve it. My wife is washing our clothes so she appreciates it much when it so nice The other children are planting cabbage as we have 1 acre of produce to take care of which we sell at the Adams County Flower Produce Auction. Tuesday and Thursday are the day's sell Tomatoes, Potatoes, Zucchinis, summer squash, pickles, hot peppers, cabbage, red beets, green beans, Indian corn. We also have asparagus and Grapes a few other things. We have about 70 chickens so we sell eggs to. I heard you have a little one now Hope she is doing good for you. They grow up so fast I always wonder if we take enough time with our children I will close this off wishing you the best with your little one, and the unknown future. I think of you often. Keep looking up God is always there.

Sincerely us,
Martin F Schwartz

Many of us could learn a great deal from the Amish people. They live simple lives, but they have profound faith and trust in God. They don't get distracted by the television in the evenings, and they don't get interrupted by phone calls. Up to the point of reading the original letter Martin sent me, I'd called myself a Christian since I was fourteen. After I read that letter, I realized how far I had to go to be even close to following Christ's example. As I mentioned earlier, I've been mistreated and mocked, and I've held on to those things way too long. Years later I would get upset just thinking about the way someone

Amish Life

"The Amish broke away from the Mennonites nearly 300 years ago when differences arose among Anabaptist leaders in Switzerland and Alsace. Seeking a stricter lifestyle including the Streng Meidung, or shunning, which includes the social avoidance of erring church members. Tensions ran high and eventually in 1693, a complete split occurred. Forty years later, many Amish responded to William Penn's invitation to come to America and settle the land. No Amish now remain in Europe. Currently there are approximately 145,000 Amish men, women and children living in 22 treated me. But, just a few months after losing three kids, Martin Schwartz wrote to let me know he and his remaining family members were thinking of me, and to encourage me to keep my faith. What a powerful testimony.

The evening when we met the family was amazing. I'd expected it to be short and sweet. I figured I'd tell each member of the family how sorry I was for what I'd caused, and how I was going to do everything

states in the United States and in Ontario, Canada. There are 220 Amish settlements accommodating over 900 geographically determined church districts."
http://people.goshen. edu/~lonhs/SamYoder.html

Key elements of Amish life: separatism (avoiding worldly ways), simple life, family life, harmony with nature, mutual assistance, disciplined church community

I could to redeem the situation. That's not what happened at all. When we pulled up to their house, they were all outside on the porch, waiting for us. We walked up to the house and started the introductions. My family had already met the Schwartz family, so they helped break the ice as I walked up. After meeting and apologizing to each member of the family, I continued to say how much I regretted my decision to text and drive that horrible day, April 17th, 2012, but then they did the unexpected: They invited us inside.

They want to spend time with me, after what I caused? I pondered silently. We walked inside and sat in their living room with them. We were talking with Martin and a couple of the older kids mostly, while some of the younger kids played. Mary, the mother, was pretty quiet. At some point, though, she went into the kitchen and came back out with popcorn, Pepsi, and pies! We spent probably an hour and a half talking with them before we finally said our good-byes. I've seen them several times since then, and every time they speak to me as if we've been friends for thirty years. They show no signs of bitterness or anger, and they've told me over and over that it was God's will for that accident to happen and for me to be the driver. What amazing love!

Ten

The day of the filming felt surreal. I woke up on a sunny Sunday morning, and I knew that soon a Hollywood film crew would have lights and cameras in my house. I couldn't believe where God had brought us from a year earlier. I was twenty-three years old, and I'd just been through the worst year of my life.

Family and friends had contacted Martin and asked him if he would be interested in being a part of the documentary, but he declined. It's customary for Amish to abstain from pictures and cameras, so I wasn't surprised when he declined the invitation. He gave me his full blessing and support to be a part of the documentary, however, and I felt good in being able to raise awareness about such a major problem with the support of the deceased children's family.

Before long the doorbell rang and there they were: vans, cameras, lights, electrical cords, and people scurrying all about. "Hi, I'm Werner Herzog," the acclaimed Hollywood director said as he walked into my house with his hand outstretched. What an honor for me! Just before filming the documentary, Werner had played a role in a Tom Cruise movie that was being released within the following weeks, so it felt really weird to have the guy standing in my living room. (We later watched the movie that featured Werner and Tom Cruise, and it was really good.)

I knew nothing about Hollywood or being on camera or anything relating to the film industry, so I had no idea what to expect. The day started with Werner asking where my closet was so he could find a shirt for me to wear that would look good on camera. That's right, a Hollywood actor and director was sorting through my closet and picking out an outfit for me. Weird.

We finally picked out a shirt for me to wear and we got started. We sat down in my living room with me on a stool across from Werner. Microphones were placed around the room to pick up ev-

Werner Herzog's crew filmed me inside my house.

ery sound. Cameras were placed in several locations to pick up different angles, and Werner sifted through some notes before the interview started. He would ask a question and I'd answer. Sometimes, I'd mess up and stutter and we'd re-shoot a portion.

Later, I sometimes saw comments on the Internet saying things like, *"He doesn't seem very emotional,"* or *"He seems fake."* I never expected that to be the response people would have to my interview. I'm not a fake person, I can assure you. I've cried more over that accident than I would have ever expected. In talking to therapists over the years, I've come to realize that I've gotten to a place where I'm kind of emotionally numb. I feel deep pain, regret, and guilt, but I have cried so much in the past that I almost can't cry about it anymore. Just because I don't cry most of the time when I speak about it doesn't mean I'm not affected by what I saw and experienced that day. I'll never be the same.

After filming the long interview, they told me we'd be going out to the accident scene to shoot more footage. I rode with Werner Herzog and Cliff Schumacher, the producer. When we arrived, police officers were directing traffic, and camera crews were running everywhere. The crew directed me to a spot almost exactly where the accident took place. Knowing that I'm person of faith, Werner asked me to kneel down beside the road, close my eyes, and say a prayer while they shot some video. Over the next few minutes a couple Amish buggies and a few cars passed by.

We filmed the final few scenes at my wife's parents' dairy farm. I couldn't imagine how the crew would tie everything together, but I guess  that's why Werner makes the big money, because it turned out great! They have an adorable scene toward the end of my portion of the documentary where my wife and I arc playing with our daughter, Shiloh, in front of some cows while I'm reading Martin's letter in the background.

I've lost track of the number of times I've received messages or read comments about people crying while listening to me read Martin's letter. It touches a nerve with people around the world. Most people today haven't learned how to forgive. The prevailing attitude is an "eye for an eye." *You hurt or offend me and I'll make you pay*. The way Martin forgave me, and then allowed me to read his message to the world blew people away.

As the day came to an end, my mind was racing with all the memories I'd gained. It felt like I blinked and the day was over. I had no idea what they'd do with the footage we shot that day. Somehow, over the next few weeks, they tied it all together in an amazing documentary that was sent to forty-thousand public high schools across the country, released on NetFlix, and posted to YouTube. The name of the film is *"From One Second to the Next"*. Even more exciting for us was the news that Rachel and I were going to be flown to Los Angeles for the premier of the film! However, Rachel was pregnant with our second child, so the flight wasn't especially comfortable for her.

We arrived on a Wednesday morning and were put in a really nice hotel, right on Hollywood Boulevard, much nicer than what we typically stay in. Later that evening, we had dinner with some actors and crew members, not a typical evening for a young couple from Indiana. We were not in our natural element, but our company made us feel surprisingly welcome with them.

I would be remiss if I failed to mention the other members of the documentary cast. While in Hollywood, we got to meet several of the individuals and families that were featured in the film. We met Megan O'Dell—who lost her father to the accident caused by Reggie Shaw—and Elizabeth Drewniak-Brigante, whose sister, Debbie, was hit by a distracted driver and to this day lives with brain damage. The people just mentioned courageously shared their stories with the world. Unfortunately, at this point I have yet to meet Reggie Shaw in person, although we have messaged on Facebook. Reggie is from Utah and is featured in the film, but he could not make it to the premier due to a prior commitment to be on the road speaking on the dangers of distracted driving.

The following night was the actual premier. A driver picked us up at our hotel and took us to the fancy theater where the red carpet event was taking place. Once inside, we asked for the location of the "From One Second to the Next" premier and were directed upstairs.

At the top of the stairs we turned the corner and there, literally, was a red carpet—and celebrities. Nolan Gould from the TV show *Modern Family* took a picture with us, and we talked with Brooke Burke before being told to walk down the red carpet.

"Just take a few steps, turn, and smile," we were told. We did exactly that and the cameras started flashing. When we reached the end of the red carpet, a reporter asked me for a quick interview. We found it posted on YouTube later, and it was really weird seeing myself being interviewed. We finally made it to the actual theater for the premier, where, for the first time, we watched the thirty-five minute documentary. We were blown away. So professional, so emotional, and so well done. I couldn't be more thankful for AT&T and Werner Herzog for the opportunity to share my story with the world and make a difference. Little did I know how big an impact that film would have on my life.

We got back to the hotel and found that the video had been posted to YouTube earlier that day. It had thousands of views, but nothing to be too excited about. But by the time we touched down at the Fort Wayne airport on Friday, the film already had more than a million views; it had gone viral, way beyond what anyone had expected! Within another couple weeks it had garnered another million views. Newspapers and magazines, including *The New York Times,* wrote reviews. Suddenly, my name started popping up in news articles from around the world. I received messages from people in Aruba, Australia, Canada, and all across the United States. The messages were mostly encouraging, although I did get some hate mail.

I love this saying: "There is only one way to avoid criticism, and that is to do nothing, say nothing, and be nothing." I knew I couldn't make an impact without taking some criticism. I knew going into the whole documentary experience that I'd hear some negative comments. You can't step out into the public without taking some hits.

I really don't know what will happen with this book or how it will affect my family, if at all. My editor warned me that a few of the statements I've made throughout this book could be seen as controversial. I'm just giving everyone an inside look at my life and my story. I'm sure if I sell more than a copy to my parents and a copy to Rachel's parents, I'll hear some criticism. I'm okay with that though. For every negative message I've gotten over the last few years, I've received a hundred great comments or messages full of support and encouragement. I'm not going to be the guy who "does nothing, says nothing, and is nothing" because I'm afraid of what people will think about me. I crossed that bridge a long time ago.

The way that I look at it is that I could keep this story to myself and keep my name from being dragged through the mud, but that would be selfish. After receiving so many encouraging messages after the documentary and television interviews went out, I've realized that this is where God wants me. My wife and I have never asked for attention, be it good or bad. We've always just wanted to live normal lives and enjoy time with our families. It's been an even harder adjustment for Rachel, who by nature is quieter. I have pretty thick skin. Things people say about me don't affect me too much. Rachel's not that way. She's very sensitive to peoples' opinions. Opposites attract, I guess.

Anyway, I've fielded criticism from various people about my referring to the crash—which resulted in three fatalities when I was texting and driving—as an accident. I've gotten messages, read comments on articles, and various other things in which people have said that it was not an accident; it was a crash that could have been avoided. I agree with part of that argument. It definitely could have been avoided. However, the first part of the argument, that it was not an accident, is based on ignorance. My dictionary defines the word *accident* as follows: *an undesirable or unfortunate happening that occurs unintentionally and usually results in harm, injury, damage, or loss; casualty; mishap: "automobile accidents."* That's right, as an example it even had automobile accident in the dictionary in quotation marks after the definition. I rest my case.

Let's move on to the next issue. I see articles all the time in which people are looking at their phones while driving and they cause an accident (yes, an accident, as defined in the previous paragraph), and are put in jail. No matter what punishment they are given, normally comments from others are overwhelmingly written in anger at the "minimal punishment" received. What part of the term "accident" was unclear? Did the person wake up the morning of their accident and say, "Gee, I wonder how I can cause major pain to another family today? I know, I'll go out and take my eyes off the road while driving and see what happens." Absolutely not! Only an insanely cruel person would think or do such a thing.

I recently spoke at a public high school to approximately 450 students. I started my talk by asking the students a simple question: "How many of you have ever texted while driving or been in a car while the driver was texting?" The response? Only a very few did not have a hand raised. If we did a national survey of the same question, I'm certain the response would be about the same. So the question becomes this: If most people acknowledge that they have texted while driving or have ridden with someone while the driver was texting, why are the comments online always from people complaining about the minimal punishment to people who cause accidents while texting and driving?

The answer is fairly simple and can be answered a couple of ways. The first way is to say that people use the Internet anonymously, so no one can tell who they are. For all we know, the person writing the diatribe has never even driven a car. The next answer is also pretty simple: hypocrisy. Fallen beings that we are, we love to point the accusing finger and judge the stupidity of others. I read an article this morning about a man who caused two fatalities while driving and glancing at his phone. When the man was sentenced to a year in jail many called the judge stupid and said he should lose his job. The article also said that while the driver was in court, he was crying and telling the family over and over again how sorry he was for what he had caused. It broke my heart.

The family hadn't pressed charges; the state had taken over the case. The family's final comments to the man were that if he turned the situation over to Jesus, he would be forgiven. Wow, what a family. Not only did they not go after the man, they pointed him to Christ. Forgiveness is huge! If the family can forgive, why can't the public? The man is devastated, crying, and ashamed of what he caused. Why make it worse on him by ripping into him? It's a bunch of people sitting behind computer screens that would never make those comments to the man's face if they saw him on the street.

I've been where that man is. I've caused that accident. The family forgave me. The public crucified me. "He's worse than a child molester." "He's going to rot in hell." "He got away with it, so he'll do it again." Do they know me? Do they know what I do? Do they know that I've met with the family and promised them that I'll work as hard as I can to prevent these things from ever happening again? Do they know that I've been forgiven by the family and by Jesus Christ, but that I've had a hard time forgiving myself? I'm pretty thick-skinned, so, usually, I let the comments roll off my back, but seriously, enough is enough. I almost cried for the man who was in the article I was reading this morning. I know his pain. I know his guilt. I know his shame and embarrassment. He did not mean to do anything. He didn't go into a store with a gun. He didn't go and buy cocaine. It was an accident. Please, cut people some slack for their mistakes.

Back to the documentary: The thing that really blew me away after the documentary came out was the fact that they cut a thirty-second bit out of my portion of the film and ran it around the world on DirecTV, Dish Network, Cable television, and on many radio stations. They posted that commercial on YouTube, too. I began getting requests for speaking engagements. I spoke at hospitals, schools, and churches, explaining why driving safety is so important. But the more I spoke, the more I realized that God was using the texting-and-driving topic to launch me into a bigger arena: speaking about forgiveness, about overcoming obstacles, and about bringing beauty from ashes.

After about nine months of giving interviews and speeches, I was worn out. I was beginning to get depressed. The adrenaline wore off after the release of the film and the subsequent media frenzy. Every time I spoke I had to watch my portion of the film, and those images and memories haunted me. I was typically out of commission for about a week after each speaking engagement, due to the emotional trauma I had to relive each time. I began seeing a counselor again, and both she and my family recommended that I take a break from anything related to speaking or being involved with texting and driving. After about ten months of excitement, my "Beauty from Ashes" goal had been achieved and we were done—or so we thought.

Eleven

After about two months of being done with the whole accident-redemption project we'd started a year and a half before, we were approaching the two-year anniversary of that horrible day. I was getting increasingly anxious and having bouts of depression. I knew that anniversary was coming, and I couldn't stop it. When April 17 arrived, I left for work in the morning with a heavy heart.

"Put your game face on, Chandler. Hold it together and get through this day," I told myself. The morning dragged on, and finally it was lunch time. I decided to drive out to the accident scene to pray and reflect on everything God had brought about since that day. That was a mistake. Right there in my car I bawled like a four-year-old. I had to call my boss and tell him I wasn't going to make it back that day. I went home and spent the remainder of the day in a dark depression.

The following day was my birthday, the big 2-4, but I felt like a big zero. My younger brother was back in town from college and he asked me to go out for lunch to celebrate my birthday. About an hour before I was supposed to meet him, my phone rang. It was a woman with the speaker's bureau for AT&T.

She asked, "Chandler, do you have any interest in a speaking engagement next Wednesday?"

"You know what," I answered, "I think I'm going to pass. My family and I have decided that it's time for us to be done with that whole section of our lives. I've been done for about two months now."

"Okay. If you change your mind, let me know. The *Today* show called today and they want you to be on next week."

I looked up at the sky for what seemed to be the thirtieth time, thinking, "Are you serious, God? You really won't let this end?" I called her back and told her I'd come out of retirement for this opportunity.

The following Tuesday, Rachel and I were flown to New York City and put up in a nice hotel right across the street from the set of the *Today* show. We did our sightseeing on Tuesday, and we got back to the hotel early that evening. It hadn't really hit me until that point that in the evening that I was going to be on live national television in front of seven-million people. I began feeling a little tense. We got back to the hotel and I immediately grabbed my Bible and sat in the big chair in the corner of our small room. I was listening to music, reading Scripture, and praying, simultaneously.

"Please, God, give me the words to speak. Don't let me screw this up." I can't tell you how many times I whispered those words. The next morning we walked across the street and onto the set of the *Today* show. It's funny now to look back on that morning. I was escorted to a makeup chair, and in the seat beside me Natalie Merchant was getting her makeup done. I learned later she is really famous, but at the time I couldn't have told you whether she was a singer, artist, or stand-up comedian. After getting the makeup done I walked out into the foyer and saw a bunch of guys who obviously were part of a band.

I asked one of the guys, "Are you with the band that's performing today?"

"Yeah, we're on in a little bit," he told me.

"Oh, cool. What's the name of your band?" I asked him.

"A Great Big World," he told me. He was an extremely nice guy, despite my complete ignorance.

"Oh that's cool. So are you guys new or what?" I asked him. He probably wanted to kick me in the face.

"No, we've been around for a while. We did a big song not too long ago with Christina Aguilera."

"Good deal. Well, see you later," I said as I walked away. I just checked the play count on YouTube for the song they did with Christina, and it's just over two-hundred-million hits! Needless to say, I was not well-informed going into that day, because Natalie Merchant has had hundreds of thousands of views on several of her YouTube videos. Apparently, living in the Midwest keeps me ignorant of these bigshots in the music biz.

A few minutes later a really nice lady came up to us right before I went on and commented on how cute our little boy was.

"Who was that," I asked my wife after the lady had done the whole baby talk thing to Zander, our youngest, and walked away.

"Honey, are you serious? That was Hoda Kotbe! She's one of the hosts of the show you are about to be on!" My wife was more on her game than I was, that's for sure. Long story short, apparently I'm not good at placing faces with names, or even placing names with famous people for that matter. I was most upset about the fact that MercyMe had been the featured band the day before, but on the day we were there, it was some group I'd never heard of!

The time arrived; we were on: Al Roker, Tamron Hall, and Natalie Morales interviewed Jennifer Smith of stop-distractions.org and me.

The interview lasted just four and a half minutes, but it went well, and I'm confident it made some changes in the way people think about driving.

"All right, babe, we really are done now," I told my wife as we landed in Fort Wayne. "We've brought beauty from ashes in more ways than I ever dreamed possible. We were a part of a worldwide documentary, a commercial, and a national television show. What more could God possibly want us to do?"

We'd barely landed when I turned my phone on and found a voicemail from the same lady who had scheduled me to be on the *Today* show. "Hey, Chandler, just wanted to let you know that Katie Couric's people called me today after you were on the *Today* show, and they want you to come back out to New York City next Wednesday."

I looked at Rachel and said, "I think it's safe to say God doesn't want me to be done with this whole experience. For some reason He just keeps opening doors for me. I'm done fighting Him."

I flew back out to New York City the following week and filmed an episode of *Katie*, which was Katie Couric's show that has since been canceled. Katie interviewed me for about seven or eight minutes, and the interview was aired in its entirety except for one question and answer. I'd just finished telling her that, mere hours after I'd killed his children in the accident, Martin wanted to tell me that he forgave me.

"Chandler, that kind of forgiveness, how is that even possible," Katie asked as she leaned forward.

"Katie," I answered, "it's only possible through a relationship with Jesus Christ and the power of God's love." Those two lines were the only portion edited completely out of the interview. I was extremely frustrated a week later when the show aired. I was kicking myself for not taking advantage of the fact that the *Today* show was live. I'd mentioned God briefly, but the interview went so quickly that I hadn't found a moment, without it seeming forced or random, to mention the power that Jesus had given me during the darkest moments.

When I got back to Indiana after my second trip to New York City in less than eight days, my wife and I had a talk. It dawned on us, then, that maybe being done with the whole accident and redemption thing wasn't part of God's plan for our lives. Getting invited to a couple high schools is one thing. When you get invited to two separate nationally televised shows and you are part of a worldwide documentary, that's God opening doors.

After the *Today* show and the *Katie* show, I had several requests for speaking engagements, one of which was in Texas. I spoke to a church and a school down there, and then I also went down to Indianapolis and spoke to a company with more than 400 employees about driving safety, because they have a large sales force that is always on the road and on their phones. I happened to have a friend working for the company who passed my story along to the higher ups and the next thing I knew I was sharing my message with them. After that, I was asked by a former classmate who is now a teacher, to speak to the students of her high school. It seemed that one person after another would hear about what I'd gone through and recognize me from high school and invite me to speak to their place of employment, or that I'd be speaking somewhere and one of the audience members would have a parent who was a person in leadership at a different organization. My message spread like wildfire.

I still speak publicly about the dangers of texting and driving. But, more importantly, I speak of the love and forgiveness we have through Jesus Christ. I speak at high schools, churches, businesses, and any other place that wants to hear a powerful story of God's redeeming power and the dangers of texting and driving.

It's interesting how as Christians we go through "mountain-top" experiences and "valley" experiences. Sometimes when we're on that "mountain top" we feel so close to Christ that it's like He's physically sitting next to us. I always wonder during the "valley" times why I feel so distant from Him. And why do those times often have to last so long? Is it because my faith is weak? Is it a lack of reading His Word? Is it me choosing to be around people or things that are not ideal for a follower of Christ to be a part of? I think, from time to time, maybe a part of it is those things. But I also think that God lets us have those experiences of feeling distant so we can claw our way back to Him, and so we can search out what He wants us to accomplish. And I think a big part of it is because we're naturally selfish as humans.

It's amazing how much money and time we can waste on ourselves. Sometimes we just need a big event to change our whole mindset. After the second big accident took place in my life, I absolutely had "valley" experiences. But now, years later and millions of lives touched, I'm experiencing the "mountain top" that is emerging from tragedy. Do I have the purest motives all the time now? No. I live in a body of flesh and bones, and I will until I die and walk in heaven with Jesus. But I try the best I can to focus on others, and not so much on myself. I try the best I can to focus on the people hurting all over the world, people who live without the luxuries I enjoy here in America.

I encourage everyone who is reading this to order a copy of the book *Kisses from Katie*. It will change how you view your role as a Christian. I encourage everyone who is reading this to go to http://www.compassion.com and start

Kisses from Katie

The New York Times bestselling account of a courageous eighteen-year-old from Nashville who gave up every comfort and convenience to become the adoptive mother to thirteen girls in Uganda.

What would cause an eighteen-year-old senior class president and homecoming queen from Nashville, Tennessee, to disobey and disappoint her parents by forgoing college, break her little brother's heart, lose all but a handful of her friends (because they think she has gone off the deep end), and break up with the love of her life, all so she could move to Uganda, where she knew only one person and didn't even speak the language?

http://www.amazon.com/Kisses-Katie-Story-Relentless-Redemption/dp/1451612095

a child sponsorship, or two or even four, today! If you feel distant from Christ and are wondering how to feel closer, I encourage you to focus on other people for a couple weeks and see if you feel any different. Unless you're made of ice, you will. If you want more "mountain top" experiences, read James 1:7: "Religion that God our Father accepts as pure and faultess is this: to look after orphans and widows in their distress and to keep oneself from being polluted by the world."

Twelve

Mistakes are a part of life; that's just the way it is. Failing to study for a test and then getting a failing grade, talking to someone in a derogatory way and later regretting it, or being involved in a car accident, they're all examples of mistakes. There seems to be no end to the variety of mistakes people make. If we know mistakes are going to happen and we'll mess up frequently, what can we do about it? First, we can pay attention to warnings in an effort to avoid those mistakes. But we won't prevent all mistakes. So the way to make up for the mistake is to react appropriately.

Let's take a look at two of Jesus' closest friends as examples. Jesus had twelve disciples who were with Him for three years during His ministry on earth. They watched Him heal the blind, the deaf, the lame, and the sick. They were His go-to crew who helped Him with His earthly mission. Every one of them made mistakes, but two of them in particular really messed things up: Peter and Judas Iscariot.

On the night before Jesus was crucified, He told the disciples He was going to be killed and that they would all fall away from Him out of fear, but Peter told Him he would never fall away.

In Matthew 14:29, Peter declared, "Even if all fall away, I will not." Just a few short verses later, verses 36 through 72,

Peter is seen three times denying that he even knew who Christ was.

In Matthew 14:10-11, we have a description of how Judas Iscariot decided to look for a way to make some fast money by turning Jesus over to the authorities:

"Then one of the Twelve—the one called Judas Iscariot—went to the chief priests and asked, 'What are you willing to give me if I deliver him over to you?' So they counted out for him thirty pieces of silver. From then on Judas watched for an opportunity to hand him over."

We all know how that worked out; ultimately Jesus was crucified. Both men made mistakes. Peter told Jesus he would never deny Him, and later he not only denied Jesus once, but three times! Judas was deceived by the riches and pleasures of life, and

Judas Iscariot

"Judas betrayed Jesus into the hands of His accusers for thirty pieces of silver. Someone once noted, 'Never was so little paid for so much!' Thirty pieces of silver was an amount that was representative of something of very little worth. Indeed, in Zechariah 11 we see the people rejecting the Lord as their Shepherd. One would think this people would be thrilled to have the Lord as their Shepherd; watching over them, caring for them, guiding them. David was [Psalm 23]. However, when they were asked what this was all worth in their sight, 'they weighed out for my wages thirty pieces of silver' [Zech. 11:12], the price of a gored slave [Ex. 21:32]. Judas was willing to sell out the Good Shepherd for a pittance. How pitiful. But, before we get too smug, his mind was warped such that he betrayed his friend for money. How the two men handled the results of making mistakes couldn't be more different. Judas, after realizing what he had done, went to the authorities again and tried to return the money. They wouldn't accept it, so he threw it down on the ground and ran out. Matthew 27:5 says the following: "So Judas threw the money into the temple and left. Then he went away and hanged himself."

> or too harsh on Judas, we should ask ourselves what price we place on loyalty to Jesus. What would it take for you to sell out the Good Shepherd? Judas had his price tag, but I fear many of us do as well. The frightening reality is: There, but for the grace of God, go I."
> http://www.gracecentered.com/judas_iscariot.htm

No question about it, Judas had made a huge mistake in betraying Jesus. Peter didn't betray Jesus to the authorities, but he betrayed Jesus by telling people he didn't even know who Jesus was. When Jesus needed support, one of His best friends denied even knowing Him! Peter didn't kill himself, though. In fact, he went on to be one of the major players and leaders in the early church. He wrote two books of the New Testament, and is spoken about in numerous other books of the New Testament as well. Jesus forgave Peter, and he accepted that forgiveness and moved forward and brought others the knowledge of who Jesus was and what He'd done for them. Judas messed up, and instead of seeking forgiveness or trying to bring others to Jesus Christ for salvation, he took his own life. What a sad ending!

So how do these two men and the way they handled things apply to us? Obviously Peter is the example of how to redeem a tragic situation. He felt great guilt and shame, but he accepted forgiveness, moved forward, and did not make that mistake again. He brought beauty from ashes, so to speak. His friend, mentor, and leader was killed, but he spread the gospel message to thousands in person, and to billions through his writings.

Bad things happen to good people all the time. We each have to decide, though, how we will handle the situations as they arise. I know a man who was a few years older than me when he was diagnosed with terminal cancer a few years ago. A lot of people, including me, I suspect, would have thrown in the towel, laid at home, and felt sorry for themselves. Not this man. He started *The Cancer Redemption Project*. He traveled all over the country and the world raising money and starting homes for orphans in Haiti. He could never have had that much influence and success if he hadn't been diagnosed with cancer.

The cancer did take him, but the good he did during those final months and years lives on, and his kids will grow up knowing better than to quit, no matter what they face. I had lunch with him a couple months before he passed away. He called me and asked if we could meet, just a couple days after I caused the accident involving the Amish buggy. I was feeling down and out, but he was literally dying, so he should have been the one feeling down and out. We met for lunch, and I'll never forget what he told me.

"Chandler," he said, "I really encourage you to look for a way to redeem the tragedy." At that point, that didn't seem possible. I wish now that he was here so I could talk with him again and tell him about all God has done as a result of that accident. I looked at him and thought that if he could bring something good from something horrible like cancer, then I could bring good from something horrible like a fatal accident I caused. I want to encourage you today to do the same. Look for a way to bring beauty from ashes with whatever challenges you are facing today, or whatever you may face in the future.

Life doesn't have to end after a mistake. It takes time to work through those initial days and weeks, but if you will trust in God to provide, He will. I'm a living example of that, and my friend who passed away from cancer left a similar legacy. Jesus never told us that life would be fun, easy, and stress-free. In fact, He said the exact opposite. In John 16:33, Jesus says, "In this world you will have trouble. But take heart! I have overcome the world." What

The Cancer Redemption Project

How it all started:
"In June of 2010 Zach Bertsch was diagnosed with Stage Four Colon Cancer (colon cancer that had spread to his liver and lungs). This type of cancer has no cure, but there are chemo treatments available to prolong Zach's life. Research has shown that people receiving treatment for type four colon cancer live on an average of 2 ½ years and 1 in 8 live for 5 years. Zach and his wife, Jenny, decided not to let the cancer win in terms of the impact that it would have on their lives. Zach believes that he was given clear instructions from God 'not to waste his cancer.' Zach and Jenny's prayer is that this cancer can be used by God to spread the gospel and bring souls to Jesus.

an encouraging verse. He told us to be ready for tough times. He also told us that this world is not the end game. We're just passing through, because He overcame the world. We're looking for heaven, so no matter what happens here, if we have faith in Jesus Christ we will end up overcoming the world as well!

The Cancer Redemption Project was developed because of their passion for placing orphans in godly families and their desire to honor God."

Learn more at
http://cancerredemption.com/

Thirteen

Bitterness, resentment, and hatred are all cancers of the mind. However they're not causes; they're symptoms. Failing to forgive is the problem that causes those symptoms. When you're fired from a job and five years later you're still upset with the supervisor who fired you, you're in an emotional cage. Locked away and sitting in a jail cell in your own mind is not where God wants you to be. It's sadly ironic that when we hold a grudge against someone we feel we're making that person suffer. We feel we're really sticking it to them, when in reality the only person we're really hurting is our self.

Take an honest look at your life right now. Have you endured painful experiences? Do you carry traces of bitterness in your mind toward people due to those experiences? It can be hard to look to the future when you are struggling with a painful experience you can't let go of, or if you don't feel hopeful.

A while back I had a very unsettling experience. I was working for a relative, doing some work at one of his apartment buildings. It was a nice day and things were going pretty smoothly. I'd just gotten to this particular building and another guy and I were taking supplies to an upstairs unit. On my way up, I noticed a couple men standing outside a basement apartment. I didn't give it much thought and I headed into the building. I came back out a few minutes later and saw that one of the owners of the building was also standing outside the apartment and was talking with the men.

A few seconds later I heard, "Quick, grab the keys! We have to get inside the apartment to help Bob!" I immediately thought that they had reason to believe that the tenant was having a heart attack or maybe a stroke. I ran back upstairs, found my co-worker who had the key ring, and ran back downstairs. He followed me and we ran around the back of the building to where the other three or four people were waiting outside the apartment. Now this particular key ring had around thirty keys on it, so you can imagine the pressure I felt as I was trying to find the single key that we needed to get into this apartment while the man inside was having some unknown problem. We finally found the key, unlocked the apartment, and rushed inside.

The tenant's friend was leading the way, I was second inside, and the guy I was working with was third. We made it about five feet inside the apartment when the man who was leading the way stopped and put his arms out to keep us from going any farther. "It's too late," he said. Let's go out." That was all he said. I looked over to where he had been looking and I saw the seventy-year-old tenant, Bob. He was naked and dead in the corner of the apartment.

As we waited on the police to arrive we were all trying to figure out who knew what and when what had happened, and so forth. It turned out that the friend of the tenant usually checked in on him on a daily basis. He'd gone on vacation about two weeks before and had just

returned. He'd been unable to get in touch with the tenant and hadn't seen any lights on. "He's been trying to
drink himself to death. He was ready to go."

Those were the words the friend told us, and they're
still stuck in my head. As a person of faith, I hope and
pray Bob found Jesus prior to passing away, but the odds
of that having happened are slim. I immediately wished
I'd known what had been going on so that I could have
at least tried to stop it. The man kept saying that Bob was
ready to go, and maybe Bob thought he was ready. From
an earthly perspective, maybe he was just tired, depressed,
and elderly, so he thought he would just try to put an end
to everything. From a spiritual perspective, Bob wasn't
ready. You don't find hope in a bottle of alcohol. You don't
find peace from a needle in your arm. You find peace in
Jesus Christ.

I was working on a project a while back at a property,
and the contractors there are very heavy drinkers. A week
or so after Bob's death, I met up with the contractors at
the job site. We all happened to be in the same room,
joking around, and I cut to the chase. "Guys, I found a
man dead a few days ago inside his apartment, and they
think he drank himself to death. You guys have got to
stop drinking so much or I'm afraid I'm going to find one
of you like that at some point." They both laughed it off.

To this day I don't know how to convince a person to
make positive changes in his or her life instead of making
bad decisions that could cost them their life. I hope this
book will show you that even a horrible experience doesn't
have to end your life. You can turn a messy situation over
to God, and He will mold it into something great. The

question I keep playing over in my mind is, "How do I help someone else, who doesn't want to, make beauty from ashes in their life? How do I talk to alcoholics and get them to understand that God has so much more for their life if they would just put the bottle away? How do I express to an abused person that God can bring good from bad and use them if they let Him? I guess the answer is probably one that I don't like or have any control over: I can't do anything. I can't make anyone do anything, at any time anywhere. But God can.

As a guy, I want to fix situations. It's hard for me to swallow the fact that I can't fix other people's lives. I have to rely on the all-powerful God, and His Son, Jesus Christ, to make changes in people's lives that otherwise would be impossible. So, if you are reading this and you are struggling with something in your life and you feel like you can't get past on your own, don't worry. The Bible says to cast all your cares on Him (Jesus) because He cares for you. He said, "In this world you will have troubles. But take heart because I have overcome the world." We are not promised an easy road in this life. Bob had a hard life, and it ended in a very sad way. If you are depressed, look to Jesus. If you have an addiction, look to Jesus. If you don't have a hope other than what you can see, you're in for a bumpy ride. Look to Jesus, the author and finisher of our faith.

I work through the same difficult issues daily. When we're wronged, it's human nature to be upset and to want to hold onto those feelings. Getting to the point of forgiveness is a process. From my own experiences, I've learned that we all go through steps in the forgiveness cycle. First, we suffer the wrongdoing and we're upset.

Perfectly natural! Second, we begin feeding those feelings of bitterness and even hatred. Perfectly natural, but terribly wrong. Finally, we all end each terrible experience with one of two options: forgiveness or bitterness. In my own life those have seemed to be the three steps in the forgiveness—or unforgiving—process.

Our natural bent is to hold onto something in our mind rather than let it go, but just because it's natural doesn't mean it's right. Whether you're reading this from a Christian perspective or from a non-religious perspective, one thing is certain: harboring bitterness will eat you alive. Christians are commanded to forgive others. Jesus said that if we don't forgive others, God will not forgive us. But, Christian or not, anyone who holds on to mistreatment and wrongs and replays them over and over in their mind builds anxiety, stress, and even depression.

Obviously, different people have suffered different levels of wrongdoings. For me, a big event was when a careless, distracted driver slammed into my car and almost killed me. For the Schwartz family it was when I slammed into their buggy and did kill some of them. Perhaps you have suffered from physical, sexual, or emotional abuse. I've been through extensive counseling to help me move through the healing process, and if you've suffered any major trials in your life, I highly recommend you seek out a professional counselor as well.

The thing that still amazes me about the car accident I caused is that the father who lost three children wanted to meet me just hours after the accident to tell me he forgave me and was praying for me. How many of us could do that? Very few, I'd venture to say. However that's exactly the attitude we should all have. He didn't go through phases of forgiveness and eventually get to a place where he could forgive me. It happened automatically, because doing so had become his lifestyle. I frequently ask God to give me that same attitude. I'm ashamed that as a follower of Jesus Christ I still struggle to get it through my head that I am to forgive others without any conditions or delays.

As Jesus was being crucified on a cross He called out, "Father, forgive them. They know not what they do." It took me a year to truly forgive the man who almost took my life in the accident in 2009. The Amish community forgave me instantly after I caused a fatal accident a couple years later. They were a shining example to me of how Christ calls us to live.

Now please don't misunderstand; I'm not saying that forgiving people is fun, enjoyable, or easy —at least not in my experience. I still wrestle in my mind with memories of mistreatment over the years, and at times my anger can flare up. However, I have to remind myself of the calling I have as a follower of Jesus, and I think back to the forgiveness that was extended to me.

It's ironic that I'm writing a book on forgiveness. I guess they do say that you learn just as much when you try to teach somebody else something as you do when you are the one being taught. I don't have this whole forgiveness thing mastered by any stretch of the imagination. A couple years ago, I was fired from a job. The boss never gave me a reason. To make matters worse, my boss was a guy I knew. It was a bad situation all the way around. As you can tell, I haven't had the best work environments at a couple of jobs I've had over the years. But the bitterness I felt during the months following being fired for no reason ate at me. Every time I saw the man who fired me, I was filled with anger. The worst part was that all this was happening after I'd been shown forgiveness for taking the lives of the three Amish children. I felt like such a hypocrite! I was experiencing freedom from hatred and bitterness from a family that had every right in the world to feel both of those emotions toward me after losing family members, yet I was harboring those same feelings towards another person who had wronged me. *Well he wronged me intentionally,* I justified to myself. *My mistake was just that, a mistake. He chose to fire me after knowing me all these years! And now, to not even talk to me about it, to not even meet with me or give me a reason!*

How wrong I was to have those feelings. I'm ashamed of the feelings I had then. Thankfully, by God's grace, I've been able to forgive this man. But why didn't that forgiveness come automatically? How could the Amish community, and specifically the family who was directly affected, forgive me immediately after losing family members, while I needed months to forgive someone for something like a job loss? I can honestly say that the Amish people in general have been an earthly example of the heavenly love God shares with each of us. The way the Martin Schwartz family forgave me immediately after I crashed into the back of the family buggy was possible only through the power of God's love. They have experienced that love, and they share it at a level I have yet to attain. The Amish get a bad rap sometimes in society, but that's a shame. They have taught me so much in so little time. They could teach each of us a little more about drawing closer to Jesus if we would just listen and observe them.

If I hadn't received forgiveness, I would not be where I am today. If I hadn't received forgiveness, I wouldn't have felt comfortable sharing my testimony on the documentary, speaking to others around the country, or writing this book. Once I received forgiveness from the Schwartz family and had their blessing to bring beauty from ashes, I was able to move forward and start that process.

The Schwartz family continues to teach me things. A while back, when my wife was in the hospital with kidney stones while pregnant with our son, I went down to the hospital lobby to grab some food. I passed a large group of Amish, and several of them stared at me as I walked by. On my way back, some of the kids in the group waved to me and said, *"Hey, Chandler!"* I immediately knew something was not completely normal if a group of total strangers recognized me in the hospital lobby. I went over and asked the kids if I knew them. "We're Martin Schwartz's kids, and we met you a while back. Our dad was rear-ended again the other night when he was driving the buggy. He's in critical condition."

You have to be kidding me, I kept thinking. *They were in another accident?* Sure enough, I walked back upstairs and found Martin's room. He was in a bed, completely still, but awake. He smiled at me as I walked in. Unbelievably, Martin had been hit again! He was driving his buggy in the dark a couple nights before and a truck hit him from behind. A few family members had scrapes and bruises, but Martin had suffered the worst injuries. The strangest part of this story is that Martin's room was just a few rooms away from where Rachel was staying! I walked over and talked with their family several times while Rachel finished up her stay. Martin just kept saying, "It was meant to be." I'm still impressed that he could keep that attitude after he and his family had been hit by cars twice. Sadly, I have a long way to go to get to Martin's level.

Experiences have taught me that life is just plain hard! Nobody would ask to be injured because of another person's carelessness. No one wants to be diagnosed with cancer. No one would want to be sexually abused by someone they thought they could trust. No one wants to be told they're fired. Life is rough. One way to make it a little easier is to let go of the pain you've experienced and release it to God. Call out to Him and beg Him to help you move forward. Ask Him to help you become all He designed you to be. It's hard enough living through a terrible experience, but it's even harder to relive it in your mind, day after day.

A word of caution here, though: You can and should forgive someone who mistreats you, whether they deserve it or not, but you should not put yourself back in a situation where you can be mistreated again. You can forgive, but some people must be loved from a distance or with conditions applied. For example, if a grandparent sexually abuses your child, you can and should forgive him or her for the incredibly stupid decision, but you should, under no circumstances, allow your child to be kept under that person's care unsupervised ever again. That's just common sense. The old saying "forgive and forget" is the biggest bunch of malarkey I've ever heard. How in the world are you supposed to forget a traumatic event? It's not as though when you forgive someone your memory is wiped clean. Whether you are a Christian or not, we should all forgive those around us who, to one degree or another, have treated us poorly or even terribly.

I've been on both sides of the forgiveness issue. I've been the guy who was the victim in a car accident, and I've been the guy who caused a car accident. Being the person who needs the forgiveness is much harder. I've made mistakes in my life, just like others have. One of my mistakes was choosing to text and drive. That choice ended three children's lives. Enos, Barbara, and Jerry Schwartz will always be on my mind. I'm truly grateful that their family forgave me. When they forgave me immediately, I felt horribly ashamed that I'd held onto anger over being hit in an accident a few years earlier. For that matter, I felt ashamed that I was holding on to some really minor issues. I chose right then and there that forgiveness would be something I'd work on for the rest of my life.

When you need to be forgiven for something you did or caused, you're in a vulnerable place. Most people don't want to forgive you, and won't forgive you. It's tough because, in a lot of situations, something gets said or something happens by accident and the person responsible would like nothing more than to be able to go back and redo what happened. I would love to go back and redo April 17th, 2012. I can't, though. It's life. You get one chance, and you live with the choices you make.

Fourteen

No matter how much we may want to redo something from our past, slow down time, or pause a stage of our life, time moves on. Every day is a gift, so please enjoy it. Don't find yourself at eighty years old looking back regretfully over failing to spend time with your spouse or your kids because your work or other priorities kept you away from them. At this point, my family has been living a pretty steady life for a while now. There were more stops along the way, but I will mention just a few to make the following point: I didn't ask to be used, but God has used and continues to use me now.

I've felt a bit like Jonah or Moses from the Old Testament. Neither of those guys wanted God to use them, but in spite of their fears, He used them anyway. Moses complained that he wasn't an eloquent speaker, and Jonah disobediently fled from God, because he didn't feel like following the instructions he was given. I'm not comparing myself to either of those giants of the faith; I'm simply making the point that God regularly uses people to accomplish His will, although some of those people require a lot of convincing.

Perhaps more accurately, He calls people all the time to be used, whether or not they want to be. Those who actually are used have to choose to accept the calling that

God lays out for their lives. I'm not anyone special or any sort of big deal. I just happened to make a huge mistake that God turned into something beautiful. All I did was harness the eyes that were on me and refocused them on Jesus Christ, the author and finisher of our faith.

See, it's not about me, you, or even Jonah or Moses. God simply chooses to ask certain people to carry certain messages to certain people during certain times. If you or I are not willing to step up and answer His call, believe me, He will find someone else. If you would have asked the fifteen-year-old version of me where I would see myself down the road, the last thing in the world I would have said was what has unfolded in my life. That's the beauty of God, though. He doesn't operate according to our schedules. He operates on His own

Reluctant Prophets

Moses didn't really see himself as a leader, but God put him in situations in which Moses had no choice but to lead. Then, in Deuteronomy 18:18, we see God telling Moses, "I will raise up for them a prophet like you from among their fellow Israelites, and I will put my words in his mouth. He will tell them everything I command him." God compared Moses to Jesus, the greatest of all prophets! Not bad for a man who wanted to hide in obscurity.

God wanted Jonah to warn the evil Assyrians (Nineveh was the capital city of Assyria) to repent before judgment befell them. Jonah didn't like the Assyrians, so he chose to disobey. He went for quite a ride before he finally agreed to obey.

time and His own schedule. I want to encourage anyone reading this who is going through hard times to look for a way to turn your situation into a good thing. Earlier I mentioned my friend who passed away from cancer a few years ago, and that prior to his passing he went to Haiti and started an orphanage. Cancer is a horrible thing, and ultimately it took my friend. But even in the depths of his pain and suffering, he turned his situation into something beautiful. I almost died in a car accident, and then I caused deaths in a car accident, and even so God redeemed the situation to bring beauty from ashes. If He can do that in my life, He can do something similar in your life.

We have friends and families who have had miscarriages and other childbearing difficulties, and it breaks our hearts. We know what it's like to go through unbelievably hard times, although we have never experienced a miscarriage. Whenever I speak at churches or schools I always try to make it a point to hit on the fact that I know I'm not the only person who has gone through hard times. I know people go through all kinds of things, everything from abuse as a child to being diagnosed with a terminal disease.

I recently had the honor of talking with Lynne Ford at the WBCL studios[1] in Fort Wayne, Indiana. She was interviewing me about the struggles I've experienced over the last few years, and I shared with her that I've learned so much from the Amish family that I ran into three years before. I told her I couldn't believe how quickly

1 http://www.wbcl.org/media-manager/distracted-driving-1

they forgave me. They wanted to meet me immediately and tell me they were praying for me.

Over the last year or so, things have slowed down a little bit for our family. I was contacted probably about a year ago to be a part of a book that was in the process of being written about the Amish faith and the way they act toward others. I recently received a copy of *The Heart of the Amish,* which was written by my friend Suzanne Woods Fisher. I was honored to write a recommendation for the book and to have my story included in the book as well.

I've also been blessed with the opportunity to share my story on another platform as well in writing this book. I signed a book deal with Hartline Literary Agency out of Pittsburgh, Pennsylvania. Joyce Hart is Suzanne Woods Fisher's agent. I was referred to her by Suzanne, and I was fortunate enough to be added to her team once she heard the details of my story! I'm constantly amazed by the way God works in our lives.

The third thing that has been happening is a plan for me to rejoin the team with Parkview Hospital's "Don't Text and Drive" campaign out of Fort Wayne, Indiana. I'll be meeting with them for a final time in a few weeks to get everything set in stone, but I'm excited to be getting back out and speaking to schools and organizations about the dangers of distracted driving, forgiveness, and overcoming obstacles. God's not dead; He's surely alive.

Despite all the positive things that have been taking place over the last two months, I've had to deal with a very difficult issue. I actually didn't even realize how far down this particular path I'd gotten until recently. Now that I can look back on where I was, I can see how bad things were. A few months back, I was in a severe depression and had been for some time without even realizing it. I'd been through so much counseling and various therapies that I was thinking things were good to go. What I didn't realize, however, was that the guilt I lived with every day over what I'd caused still haunted me. And the guilt caused stress in my life, which in turn caused health complications. It was a vicious cycle.

I'd gotten really good at hiding things from my friends and family. My wife didn't even know what I was thinking and feeling. I wanted to die. It's sad for me to have to admit that I was having suicidal thoughts a few months ago. My faith in Jesus Christ is what kept me from harming myself. The Bible talks about our bodies being the temple of the Lord, and whoever harms the body the Lord will harm.

I was so convinced I was a terrible person that I didn't want to see other people. I purchased precious metals, put them in a safe in my basement, and bought a gun. I didn't want anyone bothering my family anymore, and I didn't want anything to do with society. I see now how mixed up my mind had gotten after going through the events I experienced. I felt trapped. I wanted to die, but I couldn't! I lived through a terrible accident that I should have died in, and then went on to cause a horrible accident. I just kept asking God why I couldn't have just died in the 2009 accident.

About two months ago I started counseling again. It's been amazing to see God change my heart and my thoughts. Just a week after doing the first session, my whole world seemed different. I began "casting my cares on Him because He cares for [me]." I began realizing that I'd been forgiven by the family, and I'd been forgiven by God, but I hadn't really forgiven myself. It was eating me alive. I finally began forgiving myself, and turning things over to God that I'd never been strong enough to deal with by myself anyway.

I'd always felt that if I "moved on," I was letting myself off the hook. *The family can't just move on, so why should I be allowed to?* I began working toward a place where I could feel comfortable moving forward in life without forgetting what happened. I realized I didn't need to live every day in regret and shame. I am forgiven! Forgiveness is life-changing for anyone, especially if a person needs to be forgiven for something as catastrophic as what I caused.

I want to encourage anyone out there who is dealing with something in their life to seek God's direction. Individuals aren't strong enough to deal with events on our own. We need the love and support of those around us and, ultimately, God's help. I was holding things inside that Jesus was pleading for me to hand over to Him. If you are holding on to hurts, pains, or regrets, cry out to Jesus and ask Him to help you with the load you're carrying. He would love nothing more than to grant that request!

At this stage of my life, I'm blessed to have a beautiful wife, Rachel, a beautiful little girl, Shiloh, and a ball of energy who happens to be my son, Zander. We still live near the Bluffton area, and we still remember the Schwartz family. I stop out and see them from time to time also. I'm just a normal guy whose life includes some very abnormal events.

Every person's life goes through stages. From 2009 to 2014, our family had a horrible ride that was full of bumps and hills and valleys. Lately, after all of the drama we've experienced, I appreciate the more boring times.

We almost don't know what a normal life is like. Our kids are our main focus now, after God, that is. After all, without God, I wouldn't be where I am today. I hope that throughout this book you saw God working and moving in our lives. But you know what? He can and will do the same thing in your life. As I mentioned earlier, all God asks for is our willingness to serve Him in good times and bad. He doesn't change. He's not going to be there for you one day and completely desert you the next.

While I was growing up and enjoying all the fun things middle class kids enjoy, God was there. That same God was there with me while I was having suicidal thoughts and wishing I could die. One of my favorite musicians is Christian rapper KJ-52. In a few of his songs he has these lyrics: "It's still one love, one God, and only one way." No matter where life takes me, I always try to remember those simple words. As I've experienced, I can lose everything in an instant, but God is still there for me. He's the only constant in my life. Emotions swing, health comes and goes, and politics are chaotic at best.

It's amazing to go to other countries to serve with a mission team for a week or two. Often, the people of those countries are more joyful than we are in America—and in many cases they have next to nothing! It just goes to show that it's not what we possess or what we look like that brings happiness. True joy comes from enjoying every day we're blessed with and pointing others to Jesus Christ. As we finish this book up I'm well that I'm a flawed person. I've shared my mistakes, and I've shared real testimony about how I've messed things up even after being forgiven for horrible choices I made. I'm not trained in psychiatric treatment or in neurological medicine. I'm a guy who has played the metaphorical cards God has dealt me. I think Dave Ramsey said this: "A man with an experience is not at the mercy of a man with an opinion." I pray you will think about and process the things I've talked about throughout this book. I'm simply sharing real life events with you so that you can focus on the big picture in life. As singer and songwriter Jamie Slocum sang, "Don't give up, and don't give in. This is a race that you can win."

God bless.

Chandler Gerber

Afterword

Pain and misfortune are inevitable throughout life. You will experience different events than what I've experience and your children will experience different events than what you will experience. We don't get to choose what kinds of pain we will go through, but we do get to choose how we respond. The old cliché comes to mind: "It's not how many times you get knocked down that matters, it's how many times you stand back up." As I've mentioned, you have two basic options when you fall upon tough times. The first option is to stay on the ground while you whine and complain. Hardly a good place to stay. The second option is to stand up, look around you, and move forward. I'd be lying if I said that the average person feels like standing up after a horrible situation occurs. Nobody feels like standing up and dusting themselves off, but successful people do what is uncomfortable. I've heard it said that the best advice for the average person is to not be average. Sounds great, right? How do we get past the average part of ourselves that we each have, though? It's tough, but we can each get there.

In order to find success in life, you have to have a desire to be successful, not average. Look around you. Each of us leaves our homes in the course of a day and we bump into people who work their nine hours each day, put a little money away for retirement, watch their kids' ball games, goes to bed, and repeats the process the next day. There are a few more details in the schedule than what I just mentioned, but you get the point. Most of us are just surviving day to day so that we can wake up the next week and survive day to day again. The cycle must be broken! We were created for more than survival; we were made to do great things. Ask any child what they want to grow up to do and I'd venture to say that not one of them will tell you that they want to work forty or fifty hours a week, pay bills, and take a vacation each year. They are more likely to tell you that they want to be a doctor, baseball player, firefighter, astronaut, or movie star. So how do we get from superstar dreams to average Joe? Life happens. As you grow up and begin going through school, you face bullies, arrogant teachers, and even "real life" direction from parents and friends. That's not to say that we should all be trying to be glory hogs who only want attention, but we are not told by God to be a part of the status quo. Success is a funny word that really doesn't have a universally understood definition. One man might feel successful to have a job he enjoys and a wife. Another man might feel successful with those same things, but at the same time, be aiming for more. It's not wrong to be discontent as long as you focus that discontentment on the proper things. Being discontent with your current home is not a good place to be. Being discontent with the coach of your daughter's volleyball team and offering to coach next season is positive discontentment. There is a difference. Back to Mr. Average. I'm not saying that the guy with a job, a wife, and a kid who works at a job and takes his yearly vacation needs to be discontent with his life. I'm saying that he can be discontent with the fact that children are starving around the world so he gets involved in a local ministry and feeds the homeless. That man is a superstar. I'm not saying that the woman who teaches English at the local high school should be discontent with her life. Maybe she sees a few students in each class who need some extra help so she offers free tutoring for a couple hours after school each day. That lady is a superstar. Sure, maybe when we are kids we dream of being some awesome superstar who plays ball in front of millions of viewers, but the reality is, we can each be superstars to the people around us and to people all over the world by simply helping out above and beyond the basic survival needs of our families. Don't ever feel content to live your life, provide for yourself, and take care of your family. Don't get me wrong, those are all great things that absolutely need to be focused on. I'm saying that in addition to those things look for ways that you can change people's lives! You might be a talented pianist, math whiz, or golfer. Use your talent to benefit other people. When I experienced the tragedies that I went through regarding the automobile accidents, I realized that I could not experience a truly full life if I stayed knocked down. I prayed that I could be used and God opened doors and opportunities that I never could have dreamed of.

There are two kinds of people in the world: Victims and achievers. The reality is that the same scenario could happen to two different people and one would respond as a victim and the other would respond as an achiever. I posted on Facebook a while back that we each control our own futures, and that we each are where we are today as a result of the choices we have made. It completely blew my mind that I posted that as a bit of encouragement for people who were struggling and yet I saw comment after comment from people who said that they couldn't believe that I could post something like that. How dare I tell people to move past painful experiences? Who am I to encourage people to push through bad times in search of the bright future that God could give them? I'll tell you one thing, I've been there. I speak from personal experience. I don't write and talk as an academic with a slick theory, I lived this stuff. It wasn't fun at all and I would never wish it on anyone, but when people tell me that I don't know what it's like to be looking up from the bottom of the barrel, I want to scream. Ironically, I could tell who the "victims" were and who the "achievers" were from the comments after my post. Each of us can either cry the blues for the rest of our lives after a traumatic experience, or we can try to harness the experience to lead others to better places. The choice is yours, and the choice is mine. Life is too short to spend it complaining about other people and the successes or failures they have or haven't experienced. I have responsibility over how I live my life, and I will continue to choose the path of enlightenment and encouragement.

Appendices

Post-Traumatic Stress Disorder

I want to expand on my struggle with Post-Traumatic Stress Disorder (PTSD) and depression so that those who have experienced or are currently experiencing either of those disorders can gain some insight into how I've dealt with them. I've come to realize how common both of these disorders are, and that they can occur among people from all walks of life. After I suffered the brain injury in 2009, life became very challenging for the next twelve months as I dealt with PTSD.

I was released from the hospital after about a month, and at that point it all began. I'll never forget the first time deep anxiety entered my life. I'd been released from the hospital for a few weeks and Valentine's Day was nearing. At the time, we owned a triplex apartment building. We lived in a two-bedroom apartment in the bottom half of the building, and we rented out two one-bedroom apartments upstairs.

One day, I was in our home and I was talking with a tenant who had just moved out. She told me something about her toilet acting up and not flushing right. She suggested I take a look at it before renting out the apartment again. I went upstairs to take a look at the toilet. I couldn't find anything wrong with it just by looking at it, so I decided to flush it. What a mistake! Immediately the toilet backed up and overflowed. The water-stop valve was so rusty and corroded that I had quite a bit of trouble getting it stopped. By the time the water was finally shut off, the toilet had been overflowing for several minutes. I went back downstairs and to my horror found water pouring through our bathroom ceiling. I realized that my bathroom was directly underneath both upstairs bathrooms. I stood in the small hallway and gazed upon what I perceived as more chaos. My mind began to race. I couldn't deal with this! Such a small, albeit annoying, issue turned my whole world upside down.

My wife suggested we go stay at a hotel for the night as a little getaway for Valentine's Day, so I agreed. We made a few phone calls and got people lined up to get things dried out and replaced and we headed up to Fort Wayne. We dropped off our bags in our hotel room and went down to the hot tub. The following day for lunch we went to the Olive Garden and sat in a booth in the back of the restaurant. About halfway through our meal, suddenly it hit. I felt like my wife, the server, and the other customers were moving and talking in slow motion. It was a feeling I'd never had before. At the same time, thoughts about our bathroom, the upstairs bathroom, our ceiling, the flooring upstairs ... and on and on began racing through my mind. I started to panic. Rachel sensed something was wrong. After trying to describe what I was feeling, she said she'd take care of the bill and that I should go to the car. Needless to say, our night out on the town didn't go very well.

Over the following weeks, my wife slowly began noticing that I was having more and more abnormalities in my thinking. I couldn't process memories that I had as a child—even good memories—without breaking down and sobbing. I was unable to think about past experiences without coming to the realization that I could never get that time back. I thought back to family vacations, sporting events, and camping trips that all took place while I was growing up, and I grew depressed that I was then living through a nightmare, and I wished I could go back to when I was a kid. A few months before, I was happy with life. I was newly married, we both were working and enjoying things. After the accident, I was miserable.

I loved my wife, but at the same time, my mind would drift back to memories from the past and I would wish I could relive those times. I didn't want to go to work or even outside. I hated life. Can you relate to those feelings? I'd never had anything like that before the head trauma, but suddenly those feelings became my new reality. The thought of waking up in the morning and dealing with feelings of sadness, despair, and depression was horrible. Even more troubling was the toll my struggle was taking on my wife. She had been married to me for seven or eight months when all of these feelings began occurring. I felt as if life was moving in slow motion all around me, but my mind was running in fast forward. I couldn't process things and I felt out of control.

It was very humbling to have to go through counseling sessions. It's only crazy people who need this stuff, I thought. Great, now I'm one of them. If I had a nickel for every time I had that thought I'd be a wealthy man! I had a hard time accepting the fact that people need help from time to time to deal with the traumatic things that life can bring. Amazingly, I began looking forward to the counseling sessions. I could express my thoughts and feelings and get direction on how to better deal with them.

If you or someone you know is going through PTST or depression, please seek professional guidance. If I hadn't, I don't know where I'd be today. I had to fight through my embarrassment and pride and actually acknowledge the fact that I was going down a path that was going to lead to nowhere good. The weird thing that I found was that I'd begin to feel great after a few sessions, so I would cancel the next appointment. Then I found myself right back where I'd started. I realized that consistency is key with counseling. Even to this day, I still talk with a counselor for guidance on how to deal with issues. The goal is to find someone who is aligned with your core beliefs. You need guidance from someone who relates to you well on a spiritual, emotional, and psychological level. The bottom line is, if you are suffering from a psychological condition like I did, please don't be embarrassed to seek help.

Distracted-Driving: Statistics and Resources

According to the U.S. Department of Transportation, DISTRACTION.GOV website,[2]

> Distracted driving is any activity that could divert a person's attention away from the primary task of driving. All distractions endanger driver, passenger, and bystander safety. These types of distractions include:

- Texting
- Using a cell phone or smartphone
- Eating and drinking
- Talking to passengers
- Grooming
- Reading, including maps
- Using a navigation system
- Watching a video
- Adjusting a radio, CD player, or MP3 player

---

2 http://www.distraction.gov/stats-research-laws/facts-and-statistics.html

In 2013, 3,154 people were killed in motor vehicle crashes involving distracted drivers.

At any given daylight moment across America, approximately 660,000 drivers are using cell phones or manipulating electronic devices while driving, a number that has held steady since 2010.

This website also links to each state's laws regarding distracted driving. It summarizes the laws as follows:

Currently, 46 states, D.C., Puerto Rico, Guam and the U.S. Virgin Islands ban text messaging for all drivers. All but 5 have primary enforcement. Of the 4 states without an all driver texting ban, 2 prohibit text messaging by novice drivers, 1 restricts school bus drivers from texting.

14 states, D.C., Puerto Rico, Guam and the U.S. Virgin Islands prohibit drivers of all ages from using handheld cell phones while driving.

Those are just a few snippets from this very informative website. Take a look and be amazed, and perhaps alarmed. I urge to take the pledge at this site: http://www.distraction. gov/take-action/take-the-pledge.html.

According to the Centers for Disease Control and Prevention (CDC),

A 2011 CDC study compared the percentage of distracted drivers in the United States and seven European countries: Belgium, France, Germany, the Netherlands, Portugal, Spain, and the United Kingdom. Overall, the study found that a higher percentage of U.S. drivers talked on the phone and read or sent emails or texts while driving than drivers in several other European countries.[3]

Also, according to the CDC website,

There are three main types of distraction:

- Visual–taking your eyes off the road,
- Manual–taking your hands off the wheel, and
- Cognitive–taking your mind off of driving.

Distracted driving activities include using a cell phone, texting, and eating. Using in-vehicle technologies (such as navigation systems) can also be sources of distraction. While any of these can endanger the driver and others, texting while driving is especially dangerous because it combines all three types of distractions.

We can do better; let's pledge to end these dangerous-driving activities.

A list of helpful websites:

http://www.distraction.gov/
http://www.cdc.gov/Motorvehiclesafety/Distracted_Driving/index.html
https://www.osha.gov/distracted-driving/index.html
http://www.nsc.org/learn/NSC-Initiatives/Pages/distracted-driving.aspx?var=mnd

---

3 http://www.cdc.gov/features/dsdistracteddriving/index.html

http://www.enddd.org/
http://www.fmcsa.dot.gov/driver-safety/
distracted-driving
http://www.ghsa.org/html/issues/distraction/index.
html
http://www.consumerreports.org/cro/magazine/
2013/06/tech-aids-can-reduce-distraction/index.htm
http://www.itcanwait.com/all

Some Thoughts on the Bible's Message of Forgiveness

I'm a Christian; I should be an expert on the subject of forgiveness. After all, forgiveness is a—we might even say *the*—primary theme in Christianity. One becomes a Christian by accepting God's gift of forgiveness. Yet, as a Christian, I had a lot to learn about forgiveness. Experiences have also taught me that many—perhaps most—other Christians also need to learn a lot more about being forgiven and forgiving others.

We're sinners. Some of us are sinners saved by God's grace, but we're all sinners, living in a fallen world where sin is common and forgiveness is sorely needed. So let's take some time to learn more about what the Bible has to say about forgiveness.

Before we look at being forgiven, I think we need to establish that *everyone* needs to be forgiven. The apostle Paul wrote the following to the church in Rome:

> But now apart from the law the righteousness of God has been made known, to which the Law and the Prophets testify. This righteousness is given

through faith in Jesus Christ to all who believe. There is no difference between Jew and Gentile, for all have sinned and fall short of the glory of God, and all are justified freely by his grace through the redemption that came by Christ Jesus. – Romans 3:21-24

All have sinned. What exceptions are implied in the term *all?* _____

And how are *all* (anyone) *justified?* _____

_____

Paul also wrote this to the church in Ephesus: "In him we have redemption through his blood, the forgiveness of sins, in accordance with the riches of God's grace" (Ephesians 1:7).

Redemption through Christ's blood provides what? The

_____

Sins formed the barrier that stands between any human and the sinless God. But God said through His prophet Isaiah, "I, even I, am he who blots out your transgressions, for my own sake, and remembers your sins no more" (Isaiah 43:25). And, as we saw in Ephesians 1:7, He did that through the blood of His Son, when He died on the cross.

But the Christian life doesn't just begin with forgiveness. Do forgiven Christians still sin?

If you look back at what Paul wrote to the Romans in 3:23, how did he define sin? _____

_____

If God's glory is based on His perfect holiness, and sin is falling short of His glory, then how common would you say sin is, even among believers?

highly uncommon fairly common very common, but decreasing with maturity

So, let's say you messed up—you sinned—perhaps in a big way, like I did when I ignored the law against texting while driving. Do you find it hard to face God with your sin? _____

I did.

Do you want to hide from God? _____

I did.

Do you want to try to cover up your sin and pretend it never happened? _____

I was tempted to do that.

Actually, that pattern of shame, denial, and cover-up started long before you committed your sins or I committed mine. When Adam and Eve sinned, they felt shame, so they tried to hide from God. Then then they tried to hide the evidence and deny their blame. (Read Genesis 3.) We don't have to do that.

Read 1 John 1:9. What did the apostle John say a believer should do about his or her sins?

_____

_____

The cure for sins is not hiding, cover-up, or denial. The cure is confession. God does not expect perfection from us; He provided that through His Son. But He does expect honesty. Own up to your sins. Then, what can we do to see our lives change so that we don't need to confess so frequently? Read and summarize Hebrews 4:16 on the line below:

_____

_____

If you have trusted Christ's payment for your sins, you can approach God with confidence, even after you have sinned! In fact, that's especially the time to do so. But approach Him daily, with confidence, knowing that He wants to transform your life. Expect Him to change you. Work with Him, and not against Him. As you do, remember these words the apostle John also wrote: "My dear children, I write this to you so that you will not sin. But if anybody does sin, we have one who speaks to the Father in our defense—Jesus Christ, the Righteous One" (1 John 2:1). God does not want you to sin, but He knows it still happens. When it does, Jesus speaks on your behalf.

So the vertical relationship is settled. What about horizontally? That is, what about relationships with other people?

That's often trickier, more difficult, because although other people have far less reason than God has to be demanding, we still tend to do just that. We demand justice—on our terms. The perfect God is always ready, willing, and able to forgive imperfect people, but imperfect people often refuse to forgive other imperfect people. In the space below, describe a time when you struggled to forgive someone who hurt or offended you, or when someone refused to forgive you.

How did you feel when you finally forgave that person? (If you never have forgiven that person, will you do so now?) Or if, after a long time, that person you hurt finally forgave you, how did you feel?

Read the following verses: Matthew 5:44; Matthew 18:21-22; Mark 11:25; Luke 6:37; Romans 12:19; Ephesians 4:32; Colossians 3:13; 1 Peter 3:9. In the space below write out, based on these passages, your understanding of the Christian view of forgiveness toward other people.

Does God want us to forgive based on the other person's goodness?

Does God want us to forgive based on the other person's infrequency of sins?

Why should we forgive others who hurt us?

Based on the verses above, what are some benefits to be gained from forgiving?

Will you sign this pledge?

I _____, will pray daily for God to make me a more forgiving person.

Amish Views on Forgiveness

Six years before my carelessness ended the lives of three Amish children in Indiana, Charles Carl Roberts entered an Amish schoolhouse in Lancaster County, Pennsylvania, and shot ten girls before killing himself. Five of the girls survived; the other five died from their wounds. Not long before, Roberts' first child, a girl, had died twenty minutes after birth. He was angry at God, so he sought a way to vent his anger. After ordering all the adults and boys in the little one-room school to leave, Roberts told the ten remaining girls, "I'm angry at God, and I need to punish some Christian girls to get even with him."

Ironically, this man who needed God's forgiveness felt God had offended him, and he was not about to forgive the One who owns all life. That's how twisted one's thinking can become in holding onto a grudge.

Because Roberts killed himself, the family members of his victims were unable to forgive him directly, but they went out of their way to extend grace to Roberts' family members.

In an interview on National Public Radio,[4] Professor Donald Kraybill, of the Young Center for Anabaptist

---

4 The Amish Culture of Forgiveness, http://www.npr.org/templates/story/story.php?storyId=6225726.

and Pietist Studies, Elizabethtown College, answered questions about the Amish community's response to the killings. In answer to a question about the Amish people's ability to forgive, Kraybill noted their Anabaptist traditions, and added, "Many of their ancestors were killed and died at the stake, decapitated and so on. And so it's part of their response to forgive the enemy, to forgive the opponent.

They also look to Jesus as the one that they see as their example, and on the cross he says, Father, forgive them for they know not what they do."

Later, in response to an email from a program listener about not just forgiving but also forgetting, Kraybill answered,

> Well, all I can say is that the Amish repeatedly tell me—and this is over a number of years, it's not just around this event—that our policy is forgive and forget. If someone in the Amish community transgresses a regulation of the church—let's say they go out and buy an automobile—and then if the person comes to the church and repents and asks forgiveness and confesses this purchase of the automobile, the Amish would say we're going to forgive and we're going to forget that. We're not going to hold it against the person anymore.
>
> Will it be erased from their memories? Of course not. But they would say it would border on being sinful to keep talking about this and keep repeating this. So they do try to forget, although I'm sure it stays in their memories.

That's the idea expressed in God's statements in verses such as Isaiah 43:25; Jeremiah 31:34; Hebrews 8:12; and Hebrews 10:17. God wasn't saying that the sins would be wiped clean from His memory, but He was saying that He would not bring them up again. He would not use them against those who had accepted His offer of forgiveness.

I'd say all of us could learn from that.

Beauty from Ashes

Until very recently I never would have thought I'd be writing a book—especially one about my life. But then I never would have expected to be on the *Today* show, in front of millions of viewers. I never would have expected to have a famous Hollywood movie director in my house. I never would have expected to address millions of people on YouTube.

I also never expected to kill anyone. Ironically, that last surprise made all the others possible. I'd gladly give back the book, the TV and YouTube appearances, and the meetings with famous people if only I could regain the lives I took. If only…

We've all made mistakes. We've all done or said something we wish we could take back, if only…. Maybe it was a marriage that didn't work or a friend we grew apart from. Whatever it is, each of us has things we wish we could change. My big mistake was really public. It wasn't undercover; it wasn't something that happened between my wife and me and that nobody else knew about. My big mistake was on the news, providing a target for others to throw stones at. And boy, did they throw those stones.

It's weird and frustrating to search your name on Google and have images show up that portray you as a creep or a monster for all the world to see. I'm kind of obsessive, so from time to time I check stuff like that, and I always find myself hoping that such things will be removed from the Internet since the last time I checked. So far that hasn't been the case, and perhaps those things will always be there. But recently it hit me that when my kids are fifteen, twenty, or thirty, those things could still be there online.

I wonder a lot about what my kids will go through because of me. Will other kids make fun of them when they are older and in school? Will they be embarrassed because of a stupid mistake their dad made years before? I don't want to be "that dad" whose kids are embarrassed to even be seen with. I often think about April 17, 2012. I always wonder how in the world I failed to see that Amish buggy on the road in front of me. How could I have been so stupid? I get frustrated with myself a lot. Things from the past bug me all the time, and things I struggle with today get me frustrated as well. I want my kids to grow up and be happy, healthy, and fun-loving teenagers. I just hope my mistakes won't hurt them.

It's easy to look around the world and become discouraged. All a person needs to do is watch the evening news for five minutes or read the front page of a newspaper to be shocked and horrified. I was thinking about such things just this morning and I realized that we're fighting a losing battle. If that was where it ended, life would be really depressing. No one wants to go into battle knowing their side is going to lose! That being said, however, I wasn't discouraged because the reality is that Christians *will* lose the battle. But, in Christ, we've already won the war. This present world is not our final destination. Jesus Christ overcame death, evil, and sin on the cross 2,000 years ago! Can I get an amen?

Okay, I won't preach to you here, because some of you might not be Christians. For those of you who may not be followers of Christ, I want to thank you for staying with this book. Let me ask a question that, Christian or not, we all think about at times. Why do bad things happen to good people? It's a question we've all heard asked or maybe even asked ourselves over the years, right? I've experienced horrible events in my life.

I wake up every day knowing I'm responsible for three deaths because, a few years ago, I wasn't paying attention while I was driving. Looking back on that season of my life, I remember asking the question I mentioned earlier. *God, why are you allowing these things to happen? Can't you fix things? Can't you watch out for me and protect me? What are you doing?* Looking back now, I'm blown away by the grace God provided my family and me so that we could get through that difficult time. We knew people were watching us, so we decided to hold fast to Jesus Christ and not turn away, as is so tempting to do.

People reason, *"Well, if God were real, He wouldn't let things like this happen."* I understand that thinking. I can relate. But now that I'm on the other side of that time of my life, I can understand why God let those things happen to me. I'm a completely different person than I was years ago. On top of that, God has opened a lot of doors for me to bring good from horrible events. I continue to get messages on Facebook from random people around the world who have watched the film *From One Second to the Next* on either YouTube or Netflix. The messages are reminders to me of the plan God has for my life. I don't know how many lives have been or will be saved by people realizing they need to pay attention while they drive. I'll never know. I do know that God used my carelessness to show other people that they need to enjoy every day and not take anything for granted. If you haven't watched the film I just mentioned, I encourage you to check it out and share it on Facebook or Twitter.

Please be encouraged as you read this book. You may have asked yourself, *"Why do bad things happen to good people?"* The stories of my two distracted driving accidents—the one that hurt me and the one I caused—show you some answers to that question. You've seen stories of how God was one step ahead of us through several specific incidents. In the midst of these circumstances, you've seen amazing examples of others being helped and God being glorified.

I never would have been able to thank God on national television if I hadn't survived two horrible collisions. I wouldn't have been able to share my faith with millions of people if I hadn't lived through experiences that I wouldn't wish on anyone. If just one person finds salvation for all eternity because of my testimony, then I can see beauty in these ashes. God is using me to relay his message of forgiveness to the world and draw others to Him. If you are going through hard times, don't give up. God has a plan. It might take five, ten, or fifteen years to realize what that plan is, and, honestly, you may never know while here on this earth. God doesn't waste time though. He doesn't do things for no reason.

I pray that two messages come across loudly and clearly in this book.

My first message is about the value of human life. I have vowed, for the remainder of my life, to respect human life to the degree that I will pay careful attention to laws, God's and man's, designed to protect life. If, on April 17, 2012, I had paid attention to the new Indiana law that made texting while driving a crime, three precious lives very likely would not have ended that day. I pray that every person who reads this book will take seriously the grave responsibility of driving any motorized vehicle. Driving is such a serious task that no one should do so without giving it his or her full attention. There simply is no excuse for trying to perform *any* other task while driving.

My second message in this book is about forgiveness. This message is necessary because humans make mistakes, and some of those mistakes are truly tragic. Our time moves in only one direction. We cannot expect to get a "do-over" when we've made one of those tragic mistakes. My tragic mistake was plowing my van into an Amish buggy and killing three children. The family forgave me. Had I hit anyone else, it's very likely the family and friends of the victims would, understandably, not have forgiven me. I'd be living—probably in prison—under the cloud of their anger and judgment.

Worse still, those family members and friends would be metaphorically imprisoned under a similar cloud. I'd have made victims of them, too, as they would be rotting inside from the un-relinquished anger and bitterness controlling their lives.

I wish I'd never killed people. Knowing you are responsible for the death of another person irrevocably changes a person. I will always live with that pain. Every time I see an Amish buggy on the road I'll still cringe, and tears will still form in my eyes. But having the forgiveness of the Schwartz family has allowed me to move forward, and to help others, and not dwell on the horrors of that morning. I cannot change what happened, but through God's grace I can try to redeem it. I can work with Him to bring beauty from ashes.

Beauty from Ashes

The phrase *beauty from ashes* comes from the Bible's book of Isaiah, chapter 61. In that chapter Isaiah spoke for God, telling the Israelites—who'd been taken captive by the Babylonians, the dominant world power of the time—that although they were being punished for their disobedience, the day would come when He would restore them. He would bring beauty from the ashes of their captivity.

While I've taken that passage somewhat out of context, the awesome thing about God is that He never changes, and the principles by which He governs also never change. So while you or I might not be in captivity to a foreign nation, we can still claim the unchanging truth that God never utterly abandons His people.

More on forgiveness:

Suzanne Woods Fisher's *The Heart of the Amish: Life Lessons on Peacemaking and the Power of Forgiveness:* Everyone has been hurt. Everyone experiences conflict, great and small. Everyone has someone to forgive. But sometimes we just can't bring ourselves to forgive someone who has wronged us or we don't take the need to forgive seriously--not like the Amish do. Forgiving others in order to live at peace is woven into the very fabric of their faith. To the Amish way of thinking, "You can't love the stream without knowing the source. " We must forgive others, they believe, because God forgave us. *The Heart of the Amish* invites readers into the world of a people renowned for their ability to forgive. Through true stories gathered from a variety of Amish communities, bestselling author Suzanne Woods Fisher illustrates how they are able to release their pain and desire for revenge, and live at peace with others. Her in-depth, personal research uncovers the astounding yet fundamental way the Amish can forgive anyone from the angry customer at the grocery store to the shooter at Nickel Mines. Readers will learn how to invite God into their stories, apply lessons from the Amish to their own circumstances, and find the freedom that comes with true forgiveness.

Mary Selzer's *Wait a Minute!*: In our lifetimes we will live millions of moments. Each one is an experience. Experiences turn into lessons, and lessons become legacies. In *Wait a Minute!* the author takes a fresh look at everyday happenings and draws from scripture to leave readers with the challenge to discover those specific times in life where learning is obvious but the lesson might be missed. These thirty devotionals are unique, thoughtful and encouraging.